SAUL

SAUL

A comic carp fishing adventure in the rain

Will Martin

authorHOUSE®

AuthorHouse™
1663 Liberty Drive
Bloomington, IN 47403
www.authorhouse.com
Phone: 1-800-839-8640

Published by AuthorHouse   10/29/2012

ISBN: 978-1-4772-3053-4 (sc)
ISBN: 978-1-4772-3054-1 (e)

For Stephen, Jon and St George.

SAUL

Moonlight struggles to pierce the thick dark, heavy cloud. Beneath is an undulating rolling draft of land dotted here and there with small clumps of black trees, huddling together as if in fear of the dismal wide open spaces. Directly below is a deep depression stuffed with tall twisted elms and wild willows leaning out over the surface of a tiny tear shaped scrap of water. The willow branches reach so far across the still surface that they lace together and form a tortured intertwined canopy that slowly tightens a noose around the struggling water hole. Fallen branches and distorted roots are held captive by a dense clogging weed that suffocates the murky water around the edge. Piercing reeds force their way through the weed, fortifying spikes defending the gasping water from bank side expansion.

Some moonlight escapes the cloud and speeds toward the ground. It illuminates a gap in the tree line where a tight muddy patch nestles between the thick and thorny bushes that surround the waters edge.

A short glass fibre fishing rod lays supported on two thin sticks. The rear stick has a natural y shape at the top which holds the butt of the rod. A battered old Black Prince fixed spool reel collects the first drops of the night's rain. They start to drip from the rusting bale arm. Thick line leaves the reel and curls toward the soft mud where it is weighed down by a short thick tube of folded aluminium foil. The line spirals up through the first eye and over an expensive radio bite alarm crudely lashed to the top of the second stick. The line loops its way along the last length of the rod sticking to the wet glass between the rings before heading out into the dark, alone.

An unconscious unshaven face is slumped in a filthy low deck chair, the old stripped canvas sagging dangerously close to the muddy ground. The rest of him, below the face, is covered with a threadbare mud stained blanket. The blanket is affording little protection against the rain; numerous holes are allowing large damp areas to form on the crumpled clothes beneath.

The slack breeze dies and a lifeless cloying mist starts to rise on the warm water. The line at the tip of the rod quivers, droplets of water leap from the rings.

The line jerks.

A red light ignites on the expensive alarm, a light speed signal races to a crumpled top pocket and forces a single bleep from a receiver. In the thickening mist the line jerks again and two more bleeps are forced out. The body groans, unconsciously pulling the tattered cover closer to its chin. Curls of mist wrap themselves around the rod.

The line pulls tight.

Bloodshot eyes wild and staring fail to focus in the mist. The red light provides a powerful beam cutting through the suffocating gloom, guiding the body as it lurches toward the rod. The reel is frantically back winding faster and faster, line stripping from the spool the butt of the rod swaying wildly out of control. The tube of foil is bouncing frantically on the line, the receiver in the crumpled pocket screaming for immediate attention.

He knows he will never make it, he knows the old blanket will tangle and twist around his legs binding them together. He knows that gravity is about to grip him like a bear trap.

He hits the mud at full stretch still hopelessly reaching out to the rod with open hands. The receiver flies from his pocket spinning and screaming. He tries an impossible, last desperate grab for the rod. He watches the foil jam against the first eye and the thick line spring from the gyrating reel. Rod, reel, stick and alarm are all ripped away into the dark cold water.

The screaming stops.

05:05

Brian clasped both hands to his face feeling the cold sweat. His fingertips slid over his forehead discovering the start of another bruise. Lying on the thin carpet tangled in a thick blue duvet he glared up at the alarm clock.

"One of these days I'm going to kill you Tom Jones."

06:17

" **P** ond-acres Park, we have 3.5 acres of open fish stacked water. The lake nestles in the heart of a ten acre, protected woodland park. Relax in peace and quiet at Pond-acres. Watch natural wildlife or enjoy fishing our super lake." Tom looked up from the ticket he had been reading with a confused look on his face.

"You're having a laugh," Brian said looking through the chain link fencing.

With disappointment on their faces, they squeezed their tackle through the small gate in the high fence.

It was a ten-acre field with two acres of gasping lake trapped in the middle. The few trees dotted around the edge did nothing to protect it from the wind and even less to hide it from view. Shrugging off the beautiful daybreak like an unwanted overcoat, the lake revealed itself to be a seemingly lifeless weed choked puddle waiting to evaporate. Half of it was un-fishable, three feet deep and totally clogged with blanket weed, the other half was deeper and almost completely enclosed with reeds.

"No wonder they only sell tickets in advance," Brian said.

He was climbing a stubby ill looking tree close to the waters edge. From this vantage point he could see the depths of the water more clearly and the extent of the weed. The swims that he saw were tight to say the least. Landing roach would be a problem, never mind a carp of any size, he thought. He saw picnic tables, general litter and the remains of a small motorbike dumped in the margins a few yards further down the bank. A thin oil slick had leaked from the engine and extended itself a good ten yards along the bank adding a multi coloured backdrop to the collection of crisp packets and sandwich wrappers trapped in between the reeds and weed.

"There are two swims either side of those bushes on the far side that look fishable, but that's your lot mate," Brian said not disguising the disappointment in his voice.

"How far round, is there room for two up there?" Tom said from the foot of the tree.

The branch on which Brian was standing gave out a loud crack, Tom stepped away quickly allowing Brian to jump down.

"Sod that," Brian said, as he landed heavily, 35-year-old legs buckling under a fifteen stone frame. He was putting on weight; too much time at home.

Brian picked up his tackle and started the slow trudge around the lake; all carp fishermen know that walk. One trip with all the gear or two trips with lighter loads, Brian and Tom had opted for one.

"I thought your friend Russ was going to be here," Tom said, as he struggled along behind him. Brian glanced around the lake and back up to the tree that he had just been in.

"He might be here already," he ducked under a branch and they walked on. "He's fished it a few times, not many people bother because of the weed. But if he says it's got good carp in it, then you can bet your wife that it has."

"How's that alarm clock working out Bri?" Tom asked.

Tom had made the alarm clock for Brian on his birthday a few weeks before. It was based around an old Fox micron bite alarm. Tom had built a digital clock into the casing and used the original fox indicator sound. The alarm could be set for intermittent twitches, two twitches and a run or the all out screamer. Brian had been using the twitch and run setting.

"Funny you should ask that Tom," he indicated the bump on his forehead. "It certainly gets me up, but Tanya isn't too keen. Twice this week I've ended up on the floor."

He decided not to tell Tom about the dreams he had been having since using the clock, dreams of the dark lake, the rod and the blanket.

They were approaching the first of the swims that Brian had seen from the tree. Each one was a couple of yards wide, they were separated by a large clump of high bushes several yards thick. The largest expanse of open water on the lake was out in front of the swims. A few small fish were breaking the surface making rings around unlucky insects. The light was starting to improve the visibility, but not necessarily the lake.

At the same instant Tom and Brian froze. In the open water between the two swims, a large carp gently broke the surface. They looked at each other and grinned. They unhooked their tackle from tired shoulders and laid it quietly on the ground. Keeping low, they crept closer to the waters edge. They crouched next to the large clump of thick bushes that separated the swims watching the carp drift toward them. Both men crouched low; Tom reached into one of his many trouser pockets and slowly passed a few dog biscuits forward into Brian's hand. Brian started to reposition himself ready to flick out the freebie as the carp came closer.

"Hold up Brian," whispered Tom. "It looks like he's going for that bit of old crust."

Brian thought it was odd that there was a crust of bread out in the open water, which had not been snaffled by one of the ducks inhabiting the lake.

The carp turned slowly in the water submerging a foot or so from the bread. A second later it showed itself beneath the crust, pausing only to suck it in with the sound of a draining sink before drifting away again.

Tom had just finished saying 'Wow,' when the water erupted, a huge tail slapped down sending a shower toward the bank and the carp made a bolt for the weed. The unmistakable sound of a screaming clutch accompanied the emergence of a large figure from within the bush. Tom leapt back stumbling over the rough ground, colour draining from his face. Brian laughed and held back some branches to assist the man escaping from the bush.

"Russ, you gave Tom the fright of his life," he said through his laughter.

Tom rolled backwards his face reddening feeling foolish. He was the same age as Brian, but half a head shorter and a bit rounder. In contrast to Brian's short cropped ginger hair, Tom had always sported unkempt shoulder length brown. His hairstyle, along with his weight, had not changed since he was a boy, except that now he had a full beard. His wife constantly asked him to shave, claiming that it scared their two daughters. Tom had been married for five years, unlike Brian, he could not afford to buy his house, affording anything was becoming a problem for Tom. He tried to make or adapt as much fishing tackle as he could in his workshop, or shed as everyone else called it. He had made a three-rod pod in stainless steel, for his two carp rods, adapted an old golf bag to make a passable quiver and wherever possible he would make or prepare his own bait.

Russell, now free of the bush, took control of the fish.

"Hi Brian, how did you know it was me?"

"Where's your net Russ?" asked Brian ignoring the question, Russell pointed to a camouflaged landing net handle sticking out of the undergrowth at Brian's feet.

"It was either you, Chris Yates or Bear Grills. The smart money was on you." He pushed the net out into the shallow water.

Russell gave him a brief sideways look.

"Slide him this way a bit Russ," Brian said with a grin.

He pulled the net to the edge, a fantastic common stared back from the water. Russell leaned his rod against the bush knelt down and easily unhooked the fish in the net. Tom had now recovered and joined them as they sat on the bank and studied the fish.

"I can't believe you found a carp like that, in a hole like this," Tom said marvelling at the common.

Russell handled the fish, gently checking each fin and the tail. Even when he checked the mouth the carp remained passive and calm. Russell filed a mental note of the fresh spawning wound by the left pectoral and a small split in the tail. Satisfied with the inspection he lowered the net. With a subtle ripple of its tail the common faded into the deeper water.

"Why didn't you weigh it?" Tom said.

Russell stood; he was tall and thin, not so much like a beanpole, more like two beanpoles stood end to end on a stool. His long coat was completely festooned with small twigs and leafy branches. It was hard to tell where Russell finished and the undergrowth began. A dark green netting veil hung down from a brimmed hat obscuring Russell's gaunt features and short sandy hair. You could have lost him in your garden, let alone under a bush by a lake.

"Twenty one twelve give or take an ounce," Russell said as he sat back and watched Tom and Brian set up their rods.

"Really! How do you know?" Tom said.

"Trust me," chipped in Brian. "If he says twenty one twelve then it won't be far from that."

"But how do you know?" Tom said. "Don't get me wrong, I make you right, but how do you know?"

Russell rummaged in his bag and pulled out a small burner and kettle.

"Practice Tom get to know your carp," he proceeded to brew a cup of tea. "I caught and weighed it two weeks ago at twenty two six and it's spawned since then," he said over the steam.

After the quick cup of tea, Russell moved round the lake to fish by the reeds. A short while later Tom was using the binoculars to watch Russell play another fish.

"He's into another one already. How the hell is he coping with the weed? He is one strange bloke, how do you know him Bri?"

"He's a top man, I have known him for years," Brian said as he finished adjusting the indicator on his left rod. He set up a low chair next to Tom then slumped into it. "I met him when I was walking round that lake on the Farnham road."

"The big one with the bridge," Tom said.

"Yeah that's it, I spotted some bubbles and I was crouching by one of the brick piers trying to decide if it was carp, when Russ pops out from under the bridge and scares the life out of me."

"I'm surprised you didn't punch him Bri," Tom laughed.

"That was my first thought, but I noticed that even though he was standing further down the slope, he was still taller than me. As it happens he is the nicest bloke you could ever meet, quiet as you like, I don't think I have ever heard him raise his voice. Knows more about carp and carp fishing than anybody I have ever met," Brian lit a cigarette. "He only ever uses one rod and never uses buzzers. I have been night fishing with him tens of times and have never seen him put up a bivvy. He is one strange guy, but he has caught bigger and better carp than everybody I know."

Tom lowered the binoculars.

"That was another common, he held it up for me, I don't know how he knew I was watching. What does he do for a living Bri?"

"He's an undertaker."

16:08

Collin slammed down the phone causing the cup of coffee, nestling in his lap, to splash around alarmingly.

"I'm dealing with idiots; they told me yesterday that they had the pod. Now they tell me that when they said that 'they had the pod', they forgot to mention that it was in their other shop." He looked across at Susan on the other end of the sofa: no reaction there. He stood and drained the last of the coffee; as soon as he swallowed he carried on.

"And do you know where the other shop is?" He looked at Susan: still no reaction. Collin walked through into the kitchen where he rinsed the cup. Susan could hear his echo like voice. "It's in Coventry."

He dried his hands on a tea towel and placed it neatly back on the rail. In the hallway he grabbed a jacket from the hall stand and checked the pockets. More echo voice reached Susan.

"I'm going to meet Brian do you want anything while I'm out," he waited for a second or two then walked back to the sofa, Susan looked up from the magazine and smiled.

"More tackle?" She asked.

Collin could feel the keys in the lining of the jacket. He was heading for the door.

"It's just like a little rod rest thing. I need a new jacket Sue, my keys have got into the lining again. I might pop into town and get one."

"If it's just a rod rest thing, why are you so agitated, how many have you ordered?"

"One."

"One hundred or just one?"

"Just one, I'm going to test it."

"Ok, hurry up, Brian will be waiting."

Collin was half out the door.

"And Collin," she called back.

"Yes."

"Try to get a jacket that I like this time."

21:19

S aul raised the miniature light sabre above his head and brought it down in a wide arc while making the appropriate noise. He looked up into the evening sky. High up above the clouds a small jet was caught in the sunlight, it almost looked as though it was on fire. Saul knelt down by Obi One Kenobi.

"It looks like the empire has found us Obi One," he said in a harsh whisper. "They could be here at any time. Come, we have to prepare, I have a mission for Luke."

He pressed the light sabre back into Obi One Kenobi's hand and placed the completed figure into one of his many pockets. He looked back to the sky, the sun was leaving fast and the jet had disappeared. Saul sniffed the warm breeze.

"Sand-people," he said.

He checked that the small raft he used to access the island was securely tied to the roots of a large shrub. He moved along the bank towards the reeds. The light would not stay for long and he needed to set up. He had spent too long on the island and regretted waiting to see the results of the cheese. Picking his way carefully around the overgrown bank, he popped another cube into his mouth.

He stopped at the rushes and listened holding his breath, absorbing the sounds around him. A distant crash on the far side of the lake rewarded his silence. It could only be the swan, no doubt chasing away one of the coots in a bid to control the entire lake.

Into the reeds Saul went.

The reeds and rushes were huge, covering a whole third of the lake and riddled with deep channels and tiny islands linked by deep boggy ground. The reeds in the centre grew to be thick and close. It had taken him weeks of risky probing to navigate a safe path. One minute he would be in shallow water on firm ground the next up to his waist in sucking mire. The deep channels ran like a maze forming little islands and sanctuaries, all surrounded by soaring rushes.

One time, he had left it too late to find his way out and had to stay the night in the reeds, huddled up on a tiny island deep in the centre. It would have been far too dangerous to move in the dark. The reeds remained standing all year, in the summer they were far taller than a man, even at the edge. In winter they hardly died back at all, they seemed to huddle together protecting their warmth. Saul had tried to investigate the reeds by boat in winter; he managed to get down one or two deep channels and managed to find the giant swans nest. This was the same time that he discovered the giant swan.

Saul unconsciously rubbed the back of his hand at the memory. He made his way along a fallen semi-sunken tree, the branches still sprouting. Up to his knees in the warm water he waded, stepping between thick clumps of reed having to part them with both hands. They towered above him as he made his way toward one of the small islets. He stepped on to some hard ground and forced his way forward into a small clearing. It was here that he had spent the night, just a yard away from the giant swans nest.

He listened for the swan, then checked a small compass slung round his neck. He pushed on through the reeds taking a convoluted route that avoided the many danger areas. Eventually he reached solid ground on the far side of the reeds. He moved quickly now, around to a clear stretch of bank and stopped by the decaying stump of a large tree not far from an old wooden jetty. At the foot of the stump was a large rucksack, opening one of the side pockets Saul took out a collection of figures and placed them on the grass, he selected Luke Skywalker and placed him on the top of the stump, arranging Luke so that he held his light sabre above his head.

He took a camera and compact tripod from the rucksack and moved to a makeshift hide constructed only a yard or two away. The hide was just big enough to take the camera on its low tripod. The hide was made of woven branches and reed, tufts of long grass had been used to fill any gaps. Saul set up the camera, lining it up with the tip of Luke's light sabre at the foot of the frame. He plugged a long thin lead into the side of the camera and passed the other end out through the front of the hide. He plugged it into a small sensor crudely nailed to the edge of the tree stump, he turned it on.

Leaning over the sensor he plucked the figure of Luke up into the air. As his fingers touched the light sabre, he heard the expected click.

He checked the sky and surrounding tree line. He peered out across the water looking for the swan. He cleared some twigs away from the lens and checked the sensor again. Satisfied he returned to the rucksack and took out a small Tupperware box with one deceased murine occupant. Carefully he replaced the figure of Luke with the dead mouse. He made a few attempts to arrange the mouse so that it sat up, but the light was nearly gone and he was hungry, so he satisfied himself with face down with a curl in the tail.

Quickly he gathered his things and slung the rucksack over his shoulder. He took one last look around as he crouched behind the sensor. Turning it on he backed away and made his way into the wood popping the last cube of cheese into his mouth.

Alone in the long grass at the foot of the stump Princess Leia looked on in despair.

In the wood an owl was waking up.

21:55

Brian looked at the beer label before unscrewing the top.

"Where did you say this beer comes from Collin?"

"Guatemala. As I was saying Tom, I actually got an e-mail from Bill Gates himself, thanking me for the software," he opened his own beer. "So I sent him one back saying thank you for the £250,000. Not bad for an afternoons work," he took a long swig. "That's when I decided to take up fishing I needed to relax after that."

The three men were on the expansive landing in Collin's house. As it was Toms first visit he was getting the tour, which always ended with the tackle room. Brian always smiled when Collin told the software story. The facts of the matter were that it took Collin four years to perfect the software and if he had held on in the negotiation he might well have achieved double the price. Collin would be the first to admit that if he did not have Susan there to support him and push him to complete, it would have taken twice as long and been obsolete before he had finished it.

All the same, both Collin and Susan were pretty well off. Susan was in banking; her life seemed to comprise of free holidays and parties, but she always maintained that Collin kept her feet firmly on the ground. How this worked was a mystery to Brian, because Collin may have his feet on the ground, but it was certainly not the ground on this planet. Collin and Susan were made for each other; they even looked alike, short blonde hair and big ears. They were both the same height and possibly the same weight, although to say that to Susan would have provoked a vicious stare and removal from the Christmas card list for at least a year.

Collin had absolutely no concept of the day-to-day realities of normal life, the idea of physically working for a living completely eluded him. Ever since he received an insurance pay out and extensive estate following his parent's death, Brian would have been surprised if Collin's feet ever touched reality again. Still, a very handy friend to have, Collin was never shy of putting his hand in his pocket for a friend, but to be fair he had very few friends.

Most people who met Collin did not like him, because nine out of ten times he completely failed to understand the other guy's plight. You could tell Collin that your wife had left you, that you had lost your job and the dog was dead, give him a sob story big enough to make a country and western box set. He would just say something like, 'you should take up golf use your free time to have more fun'. Then buy you a large drink. Mention in passing that you had broken the handle on your favourite reel and the chances were good that he would present you with a new reel handle, if not a new reel, in the pub the next day. Possibly in a nice box with a bow on the top, if Susan had anything to do with it. Then buy you a large drink.

Brian kicked himself, Collin had helped him a few years back, getting him and Tanya a practically interest free mortgage, something that Collin never mentioned or held over him, he was a true friend in every sense.

The cynic in the back of Brian's head waved a placard silently indicating that Collin could afford, in every sense, to be a good friend.

"After you Tom," Collin said.

It was just a spare room in the house, but it was a big house. Tom looked round amazed, the room was twice the size of his living room and stuffed with fishing tackle. There was even a horizontal rack to store the rods.

"Wow," Tom said when he saw the rack. "I have never seen this much tackle that wasn't in a shop or stolen."

Brian slumped into one of the three chairs already set up around a huge bivvy table at one end of the room. He looked down and examined the chair.

"Is this a new one Collin?" he stood again and inspected it more closely starting to laugh. "Hang on this is a 'Badger' chair; that's a bit down market for you isn't it?"

"That is a good chair," Collin said. "You know me, it's not about money, it's about design," he carried on in spite of Brian's laughter. "I had to prove to Sue that carp fishing was not all about money so bought some stuff from Badger on-line; including that chair."

"I've got one of those chairs," Tom said a little disgruntled. "And it's a good chair."

"Actually I was really surprised Tom. I used it last week in a club match over at Claybourn lakes. Sat in it all day, felt good, rock solid, adjustable legs, just enough padding, thirty quid delivered to the door, you can't argue with that."

"Bang on Collin," Tom said, with enthusiasm. "See, I told you Bri," he said poking Brian in the arm. "It's a bloody good chair. Are you taking it with you next week Cole?"

"Not a chance."

"Oh," Tom said, deflated.

Brian was laughing again.

"I told you Tom, he's a tackle tart, he was spending so much money on fishing gear that Sue made him set up an on-line tackle shop so that he didn't take up two rooms in the house."

"It's true," Collin said laughing. "This is my stockroom I suppose; I get a lot of stuff in bulk, sell at a tiny mark-up which covers all my fishing. Sue thought it might give me something to do."

"I'm in the wrong bloody job," Tom said throwing up his hands joining the laughter. "Ok, what are you taking with you next week?"

"I wanted to ask Brian about that. This lake, I need some info so I can narrow down the tackle. I want to keep it to a minimum."

Brian slid further down the chair with more laughter.

"Coming from the man who wrote to Kevin Nash asking him to make a trailer for his trolley, I find that hard to believe."

Collin took a cigarette from a small box on a shelf.

"I would like to know more about the lake. And it wasn't a trailer it was more of an extension."

He reached to the wall and flicked a little switch. What Tom had thought was a smoke alarm on the ceiling was in fact a powerful extractor fan. Susan hated smoking; this was the only room in the house in which she allowed Collin to do so.

"What's this Russ bloke like, have I met him?" Collin said and slouched back in his cocoon chair.

Brian sat up serious for a moment.

"You have as it goes, he runs the firm who took care of your mum and dad." Brian had been worried about mentioning this because he knew Collin was still a bit touchy about his parents. However, it was better to mention it now rather than later, he did not want to upset Collin.

"The tall one or the short one?" Collin asked.

"Definitely the tall one."

"Yes, I do remember him, very professional I thought. So what's the deal with the lake?"

Brian breathed a mental sigh of relief, because he could not wait to get on this lake. He had heard Russell talk of it many times when they had discussed tactics and baits. Russell had some very fixed views on how to catch big fish.

Brian found himself getting quite frustrated fishing with Russell in the early days. On the majority of their fishing trips Russell would catch the better fish. Regardless of how much Brian read or spent on bait and tackle Russell consistently beat him using only one rod and minimum tackle. It would be interesting to see how Collin matched up to Russell, because Collin used everything. Collin had only been fishing for about three years, but had done little else other than go fishing in that time. He had all the enthusiasm of the beginner and the time and money to keep up with it. His collection of photos would have impressed any seasoned carp angler. He had an eye for quality tackle and no fear of quality prices. He would spend hours on the computer comparing maker's claims and prices. He wrote product reviews on all the things he bought and posted them on his web site. If there was a new theory or method, he was trying it or buying it. When he bought the korda underwater carp series, he went fishing for a week with a portable DVD player and a stack of batteries. Collin's winter boots cost a hundred and fifty quid, but his feet never get hot cold or wet. "There's no such thing as bad conditions," he would say. "There's only a bad choice of equipment." Brian's boots cost fifty quid because that is how much Tanya would let him spend. This, he thought, was a little bit cheeky coming from a girl with eight pairs of boots, sixteen pairs of shoes and two pairs of ridiculous slippers. He would have pointed this out to Tanya, but he didn't want to lose the fifty quid.

"It's pretty remote, there's the lake and a big chunk of woodland around it. It's been fenced off for the last fifty odd years," Brian said and relaxed back into his chair. "The last owner wouldn't let anyone on the land and was inclined to take pot shots at anyone who wandered in by mistake. The old man died a few years back, but it took until now to track down some distant relative in Australia, Austria, Algeria, some place like that. Russell's uncle owns most of the land that surrounds the estate."

"How do you know there's any carp in it? It might be full of bloody goldfish," Tom said from the Fox recliner.

"Russell lived with his uncle when he was a kid, grew up working on the farm. He spent all his spare time on the lake, he was catching big fish, upper twenties sort of stuff and that was thirty years ago. Had anybody else said that, I would have thought they were stretching it a bit, but not Russ, he has photos of some big carp and a few shots of the lake. It looks superb."

"What about the owner," Collin said. "Did he give him permission?"

"Russ used camouflage and stealth to sneak in and poach. The old man would drink a lot and stumble round the lake with his gun, but he never found Russ, he's pretty good at it."

"Hey, I can testify to that," Tom said. "He scared the bloody life out of me this morning. Jesus, did he make me jump."

Brian reached for his cigarettes and carried on.

"He catches a lot of big fish, you could learn a lot from him Cole. He really knows carp; he doesn't so much go stalking, just kinda knows where the carp are going to be. Anyway the whole place is a bit 'Lost World' now evidently; overgrown, forgotten about."

"Hey, how about a little wager on the side," Collin said. "Not much, maybe twenty five for the most weight and ten for the biggest fish."

"Sounds good to me," agreed Brian.

Tom shuffled a little uneasy in his chair.

"Um, ok then, but for Christ's sake don't tell my wife," Tom said, knowing there would be hell to pay if she found out.

They spent the rest of the evening watching fishing DVDs and talking tackle. Collin did most of the talking as he had most of the tackle.

23:46

I *love being an owl*, she thought, *I'm so graceful and elegant. I can swoop, soar and dive. I can see tiny objects at great distance even on the darkest of nights. And I don't make a sound in the air.*

She laughed, very quietly.

It was a beautiful night, light cloud allowed the full moon almost continuous access to the ground. She circled the lake and spotted the mouse immediately, barely using the awesome power of her eyesight. She swooped down to about twenty feet and stayed there hovering on the light breeze. Too high to alert her prey and perfect for the start of the attack run. She waited for the light cloud to cover the moon then silently dropped out of the air.

As soon as her claws touched the prey a blinding flash turned night into day. The owl reeled in shock, but managed to stay in flight. Blinded and on the edge of panic she dropped the mouse and tried to concentrate on staying in the air. She heard the mouse hit the water. She had to stay in the air. If she fell into the water, she would almost certainly drown.

Steadying her wings, she levelled out and began to circle in a wide arc.

What the hell happened there? I can't see a dam thing. Where the hell am I? Right, calm down, remember you're an owl; graceful, calm, intelligent. That's better, relax.

Ok, I can feel a slight down draft here and the temperature is lower. I did the dive, came up turned right and levelled out so I must still be over the water, good, nothing to run into over the water. There's not much wind so I'm fine for a bit. Boy I am so glad that I'm an owl; any other bird would have panicked and been all over the show. Right, now to try and get some height, height is my friend.

She beat her strong wings, lifting her higher, she made it back up to twenty feet.

That was a close one though, she thought.

There was a silent thump, the owl span down.

17:04

Tom carefully adjusted the angle of the light while looking through the large square lens. Satisfied, he took hold of the soldering iron and slowly manoeuvred it toward the end of the diode he was pressing on to a circuit board with his other hand. His forefinger and thumb looked massive beneath the magnifying glass. He moved the tip closer to the end of the tiny diode, the little blob of solder on the end of the iron started to smoke. He moved in closer.

Dink.

Everything went black. A sharp pain shot up tom's finger he dropped the iron and pushed himself back in his chair giving his knee a nasty crack on the edge of the old school desk.

"Bloody hell."

He stood and took a step toward the main light switch by the door, there was a creak and the room was flooded with dazzling sunlight. Blinded and in pain Tom stumbled toward the door.

"Mum says dinner's ready," a little voice said.

The door closed again, the light was gone and he was back in the dark. He caught his ankle on something solid.

"Bloody hell."

Tom instantly put his hand over his mouth, lost balance and crashed to the floor. He crawled to the door flicked on the main light and studied the burn mark on his finger nail. Returning to the bench the soldering iron had damaged the circuit board. He unplugged the iron and dropped it into the stand and threw the board into the spares box. He looked over at his fishing tackle stacked neatly around the walls of the workshop. After tea he would set out the tackle for tomorrow and finish the food preparations.

Tom was cooking the main meals over the weekend; he loved to cook and outside catering was becoming a speciality. When he and Brian went fishing, Tom always prepared the food. This time there would be four people to cater for and Tom was looking forward to it. He did not feel that he could compete with the others when it came to tackle or even fishing knowledge, but when it came to a good meal on the bank Tom won hands down.

17:10

Brian added the lupins, which had been cooling in one of the saucepans, to the bucket of hemp and maize. Carefully he poured in a measured amount of salmon oil and then added a kilo bag of trout pellet dust. He stirred the mixture with a wooden spoon from the draw. The other bucket was half-full of chopped scopex boilies. He poured some of the particles into the boilies and stirred. He repeated this process, pouring the mix from one bucket to the other until it was evenly mixed. He divided the mixture between the two buckets and stood them by the back door. Several of the boilies had escaped along with some of the particles during the mixing process. He made a half-hearted effort to clear the floor of obvious debris. He heard a key in the door. Quickly he swept the remaining spill under the cooker. Tanya stood in the doorway.

"Get out of my kitchen," she snapped.

Brian recognised the tone and made a hasty withdrawal grabbing the buckets and clasping several bags of dry ingredients to his chest. He made his way into the garden, Tanya's voice floated through the open back door.

"For Christ's sake Brian could you have made any more mess?"

He heard the banging of pots and pans thrown into the sink and then all was quiet. A few seconds later Tanya appeared at the back door with a blackened saucepan in her hand.

"Look; look at this, what the hell have you done to this?"

She waved the pan in the air then threw it out on to the lawn and disappeared back into the house. Seconds later, she reappeared and flung the lid out to join it.

"You owe me a new saucepan. Next time you go in that kitchen it had better be to deliver my new saucepan," she slammed the back door.

Brian looked at the buckets, crouched down and ran his hand through the warm particle spod mix he had created. He inhaled the heady vapours steaming up from the bucket and smiled. This was going to blitz the lake, he thought. The kitchen window flew open.

"What is that god awful smell," Tanya shouted.

Brian grabbed the buckets and ran off to the end of the garden heading for the shed.

17:12

Collin wiped the sweat from his brow and sat down on the doorstep. The only problem with having all the fishing tackle on the first floor was that it had to be carried down. It had taken ten trips to get what he needed down to the car and an hour to load it all into the back of his Saab. The last thing to be loaded was the bait bag. He unzipped the large holdall and rummaged through the contents making mental calculations as to how much bait he may need. He ran back to the tackle room one last time and brought down a bag of pre-soaked peanuts. Just in case, he thought.

The only thing left on the car list was to grab the unhooking mat and landing net. He walked into the double garage and took down the massive net and mat from their hook; pausing at the door he made a few more calculations. He packed the gear into the car and crossed it off the list, returned to the garage and took another case of beer from the stack in the corner. He took a cautious look around to make sure that Susan had not seen him load the extra case. Susan was not one for excess; with the possible exception of shoes and clothes, hats and bags.

He closed the tailgate and went back to the tackle room, just enough time for a DVD before dinner. He flicked through a stack of fishing titles and pulled out the fifth korda DVD. He settled back with a beer and cigarette.

17:22

In the spare room Russell opened a small wardrobe and took out a few clothes, a small bag, a rod and landing net. He opened the bag, after a perfunctory look he appeared satisfied. He took everything down to the hall and put it next to his boots. From the cupboard under the stairs he grabbed a couple of gas canisters.

He decided to pack the car in the morning.

05:41

U sing the key to pull his front door too Tom paused on the cool porch soaking up the early silence before dropping his boots into the back of the old Landrover parked on the drive. He secured the canvas flap. After a brief look beneath the vehicle Tom got into the passenger seat. Brian looked across.

"All set?" he said as he fastened his safety belt.

Tom looked up from the map on his lap and checked his watch.

"Sorted mate, its five to six now, we should arrive seven to seven thirty. Before you ask; yes, I have looked under the van."

"I know what you're thinking, but since that cat thing last year I can't help it. I have to be sure."

"Brian it wasn't your fault, there was no way of knowing that a deaf cat would be stupid enough to fall asleep in front of the back wheel. Could have happened to anyone, don't feel bad about it."

Brian looked at Tom slightly confused.

"Tom, I don't give a toss about the cat. I had to pay my little brother a tenner to clean that tyre. And I got loads of flak from the neighbour when I took the cat back. He's never been the same with me since. I even offered to replace the cat. The git made it all look like my fault. So now, I always check under the van, because killing cats is not as much fun as you might think," he reached out to start the engine.

"Hang on Bri," Tom said, stifling a laugh. "I don't want to wake the wife. Do you think we could roll off the drive and down the hill a bit before we start the engine?"

"Sure mate, I wouldn't want to upset your old lady."

They laughed and Brian released the hand brake. The heavy Landrover slid silently forward. As soon as the bonnet was out of the drive Brian stamped on the brake to avoid hitting a cyclist who swerved just in time to avoid the heavy vehicle.

"Where the hell did he come from?" Brian cried out.

In the dim streetlight they could see that the cyclist had only paused long enough to shout 'idiot' at the top of his voice. This was cut short by Brian starting the engine, flicking on the headlights and forcing the Landrover into gear. The beast made a noisy lurch forward and stalled. Brian restarted the engine, revved it several times, pulled out on to the road and away down the hill. Tom looked back toward the house. The dog was barking and lights were coming on. One of his neighbours was twitching the curtains. The cyclist took the opportunity to reiterate his earlier statement adding a one fingered gesture as they passed him. Tom slid the window closed and shrank back into his seat.

"Could have gone better Bri; could have gone better."

06:10

C ollins eyes flew open; he instantly regretted it and closed them tight. Where was his phone, the alarm tone which he had chosen at random the night before, was a repetitive irksome rasping sound. His blind fumbling was not paying off. He risked one eye, a bright light stung him. He found the mobile under the makeshift pillow and yawned in the new silence before pulling the thin quilt over his face to avoid the light. He felt a bit groggy, but better than he had first thought. He had a long stretch, actually he felt quite good and he had been looking forward to this weekend. Another long stretch, he felt great, he rolled over on to his front and straight off the narrow bed chair. He hit the floor with a thump sending a beer can and an ashtray skitting away in different directions.

He remained face down not moving, trying to ignore the pain in his nose. He lie there listening to the last rolls of the beer can on the wooden flooring, the tackle room door opened and Susan's voice descended on him.

"I thought the idea was not to wake me on my day off," she turned off the harsh desk lamp and opened the curtains. Gentle dawn light softened the room. "And clear up before you go," she paused concerned. "Are you all right Collin?"

Collin rolled on to his back still wrapped in the quilt looking up at his wife, he was grinning.

Twenty minutes later he was in the Saab, heading south at ninety-five.

06:51

T he track ended in a wide-open gate, Brian slowed to a halt and peered across the small field ahead.

"Well, it's not this one either Tom."

They had been down several of these tracks, each one had either run to nothing or just stopped dead at a hedge or gate leading to a field as this one had.

Brian turned the engine off and pushed back against the hard seat stretching his legs, then reached into his top pocket for a cigarette. Tom was trying to orientate the map using a small compass.

"It doesn't make sense Bri, either the map's wrong or the compass doesn't work."

Brian opened his door and got out. He took in a long deep breath and let his shoulders relax. The sun was starting to make a big impression on the horizon. A low layer of mist in the field ahead was swirling in a subtle breeze. The light mist was cool against his face and hands. The only sounds were the tink of the cooling engine and a single skylark somewhere above the fields. Brian closed his eyes and soaked up the peaceful land of silver dew on green leaves. The spreading sun heated the mist in the field sending it into delicate thermal spirals. Diffused rays pierced the mist and illuminated his unshaven face. Brian lit the cigarette, took a deep drag and released the smoke in a long steady plume. He coughed, spat and got back in the Landrover slamming the door.

"Where the hell are we Tom?" he slid the window open and flicked out the ash.

"Calm down, give me a minute we can't be far away." Tom checked the compass again and jumped out.

Brian watched him leave a dark trail in the wet grass as he entered the field. Tom walked a full circle then stood facing the dawn; he pointed at the sun and shook the compass.

"That's east you idiot."

He stomped back to the Landrover and threw the compass aimlessly over his shoulder as he slumped into his seat. He left the door open to clear Brian's smoke.

"Sorry Bri, we aren't far off and I know where we are on the map now," he offered the map up for Brian to see. "We need to turn round. The ground's very soft in that field, but there was a gate back down the track. If we could turn it round there, go back and take the next right, we should be there in about ten minutes."

Brian checked the time on his mobile, 7:05. He started the engine and reversed back down the narrow track.

07:20

From this vantage point Pitcher could see most of the road for about a mile in each direction; he took another bite of the sandwich before putting it back in his lap with the others on the greaseproof paper. As he reached for the thermos on the passenger seat a black car caught his eye. The car was gunning it up the hill toward him. Despite the slope, the heavy black car was easily picking up speed.

Sergeant Pitcher left the thermos and moved the sandwiches from his lap, not taking his eyes off the large car. His own engine coughed into life, he clicked his seat belt and pulled it tight. He pushed the gear lever forward, the black car shot past. Pitcher pulled out behind spraying dust and gravel from beneath the rear wheels.

Now on the road he could only get fleeting glimpses of the rear end as the black car slipped round the tight bends showing no signs of slowing.

He dropped a gear as the road tightened into the sharp S bend at the bottom of the hill. He glanced down at the radio, he wanted to call in, but dare not take his hand from the controls on this stretch of road.

"Christ," he swore out loud. "This guy's pushing it."

The sharp S bend ahead had taken its share of tourists and boy racers in the past. He had chased many of the local yobs round these lanes, but he was feeling a little old for all this and the car he was chasing was not helping the mood.

He had to stamp heavily on the brakes; the speed catching his reactions off guard, the car shuddered and took the bend wide. He prayed nothing was coming the other way as he fought to control the exit from the bend, he floored the peddle accelerating out on to the straight, flicking a switch on the dash, the siren and lights went on.

"You're nicked you disrespectful bastard," he muttered.

Russell glanced into the rear view and down to the speedometer, he was only doing sixty, he slowed. The police car matched his speed. The officer gestured for him to pull over.

A minute later Pitcher took a deep breath and walked toward the black car he looked through the engraved glass into the back and stopped. Through the glass he could see a six foot bundle wrapped in an old blanket.

This is all I need to start the weekend he thought, some nut case speeding in a stolen hearse with a dead body in the back. I am definitely too old for this bollocks. Crime isn't what it used to be, it's all weird stuff these days and the paperwork would take a month. He gritted his teeth.

The rest of the world was slowly creeping on to his patch. He knew that to solve crime you have to understand it: the evidence suggested that he did not.

Fingering the unfamiliar pepper spray in his pocket, he stepped toward the open driver's window. It crossed his mind that maybe he should have taken the opportunity to radio in before approaching the car. He used his most authoritative tone.

"Switch off the engine and step out of the vehicle: now. Do it quickly and quietly."

Russell got out. Pitcher looked up and swallowed. Yes, definitely should have used the radio, he thought.

"Right, now place your hands on the bonnet," as he said it he realised that this would be ridiculous and changed his order. "Ok put them on the roof." He felt the spray in his pocket.

Russell was dressed in light combat trousers and pale camouflage t-shirt. Could be one of those urban terrorists, Pitcher thought, he gripped the spray a little tighter.

"What's your name, where are you going and where did you get the car?"

Russell turned to the officer and reached for his back pocket.

"I'm the undertaker," he said in his deep tone.

Pitcher whipped out the spray, took an aggressive stance holding it at arms length in front of him.

"Put your hands BACK on the car," he shouted.

He felt awkward having to hold the pepper spray so high in order to have any chance of hitting the driver in the face.

"Not so fast son, what's in the back?"

"Fishing gear."

"What?"

"I wrapped it up so I wouldn't damage the finis . . ."

44

"Quiet," Pitcher shouted.

Pitcher took another look; on closer inspection it was obvious that the bundle was too thin to have been a body. He felt a little foolish.

"You could get hurt round here driving like that son."

He looked Russell straight in the eye adding the weight of the law to his threat.

In his opinion, there was only one way to deal with joy riders, thieves and people who make you look stupid. Make it clear from the start that you do not like them. Pitcher slowly lowered the spray not taking his eyes from Russell.

"Your driving licence, please Sir," he barked.

Even more slowly, Russell took his hands off the car roof and gave pitcher the licence. Pitcher looked hard at the tiny photo on the license; it could have been a picture of his wife in the nude for all he could make of it without his glasses. He would be damned if he were going to put them on, fortunately Russell was filling in the blanks.

"My name is Russell Black and I am going fishing on my uncle's farm, Tom Black's farm. Tom Black is my uncle; I'm his nephew Russell Black. My wife needed the car so I borrowed one from work. I'm an under . . ."

Pitcher held up his hand stopping Russell, his face completely frozen while he took in the stream of information. He relaxed into a broad smile.

"Little Russell Black, I think I still owe you a clip round the ear," Pitcher stepped forward and held out his hand laughing, Russell shook it warmly. "My god, it must be fifteen, no, over twenty years since I see you round these lanes. Rusty old Escort as I remember, I heard your uncle had access to the lake; I should have guessed that you would show up. After all those summers sneaking in through the back field you will finally get to drive in through the gate."

He tapped his nose. "I knew all about your little trespasses back then."

"Did Mac ever complain?" Russell looked surprised.

"Knowing old Mac I suspect he would have just shot you if he found you, rather than bother with a complaint. Your uncle must have warned you about Mac, he didn't like visitors." Pitcher thought for a moment. "He didn't like people. Mac and his wife were never what you would call sociable to start with. He became a total recluse after she went."

"I never saw his wife, when did she die?"

"She disappeared in sixty eight, a bit before your time lad. Funny story though, Mac claimed that she went shopping one weekend and never came back. Six months later no one had heard from her, so we looked around the house and we spent all day searching the wood and around the lake. We never expected to find anything, the evidence suggested that she had left him; it was a lot easier in them days to disappear and start again. I will tell you something though, when we searched the grounds around the lake, old Mac just sat on the little wooden jetty drinking from a big jar of whisky, all day just staring out across the water toward the island drinking the whisky. Right at the last knockings my sergeant made me swim out to that island. And I tell you now, as I stand here in front of you, I pulled myself on to that island, I pushed aside some of the undergrowth and got the fright of my life."

Russell leaned a little closer and whispered.

"Did you find a body?"

"No, I was attacked by a cygnet. You know: a baby swan. Damn thing took a chunk out of my hand, vicious little bugger chased me off the island. I had to swim back with the damn thing pecking at my feet all the way to the bank. It was very embarrassing. They called me constable cygnet for years after that. They call me sergeant cygnet now of course."

"I remember Mac," Russell said. "He would walk around the lake, always drunk. I saw him fire off a couple of rounds into the trees a few times. He always struck me as a very angry man; I just kept out of his way."

Pitcher realised that he was still holding the spray loosely in his hand, he returned it to his pocket.

"Sorry about that, it's pretty harmless. I've carried that spray for ten years and never had to use it, not once, waste of time. Give me a truncheon any day; I used one of them all the time. If I get the chance I will pop down tomorrow and be a bit more sociable."

They wished each other well and Russell went on his way. Pitcher returned to the hill to finish the sandwiches, his thoughts marching toward retirement.

07:46

Brian switched off the engine glad of a rest from the revving two point five-litre diesel. He looked down at his feet, the trainers he wore for driving were thick plates of mud. The clay had worked its way up the inside of his trouser legs.

When they had reversed into the gateway, in order to turn around, the ground had looked fine. Nevertheless it had taken; pushing shoving swearing, four-wheel drive two wheel drive, swearing shouting, hi gear low gear, digging swearing again and finally some traction, an hour to get back out again. The sun had left the horizon and the mist had evaporated taking all the romance of dawn with it.

He looked across at Tom standing by the open passenger door and started to laugh. Tom looked down at himself he was covered in sloppy mud and grass. The wet mud had soaked through his fleece and T-shirt he could feel the weight of it on his trousers. His face and hands were filthy and the clay had completely encased his feet. If he were to lie on the ground face up, he would have disappeared.

"Well like I said Bri, we just turn round by this gate and we should be there in ten minutes."

He was grinning through the mudpack

08:11

Saul pushed the polarised glasses up on to his forehead and rested his back against the trunk. He paused to enjoy the early sun on his face and glanced around the lake perimeter picking out some movement deep within the reed bed. The reeds were too high to see what was disturbing them at their root. It must be the swan, in the distance he could hear dogs barking. Where they lived, he had no idea. There was not a home for miles, other than the farm.

He looked out beyond the lake over the wood, thick trees sprawled out for many acres surrounding the lake. All the trees were in full leaf, the old house was barely visible nestled amongst them. A soft breeze was rolling down from the house over the trees bringing the faint smell of the abandoned garden.

The island was big enough to support a few short trees and tall shrubs. The bushes and shrubs overhung the bank on three sides, the fourth was dominated by the tall dead tree in which Saul was perched. It stuck in the ground like a giant tooth from some deranged Jurassic beast. All of the tree's branches and leaves had been lost decades before. The rest is completely denuded of bark, the bare bleached trunk hardened by the sun then splintered and cracked by occasional lightning attracted to its height. Saul was sitting astride what was left of one of the upper most boughs. At the base of the trunk the bank was clear like a beach, only a few owl feathers cluttered the bare surface.

Over the years, the trunk had leaned out over the water. This made it easier to climb and meant that Saul was directly above the fish he had been watching. Water vapour was rising from the tops of the trees in the early sun. Hundreds of birds were dashing across the skyline on important bird business. He wondered for a moment what it would be like to be a bird, he dismissed the thought, birds were stupid.

The rising water vapour gave the impression of a tropical landscape or with a little more imagination, an alien one. Saul was lost in this for a few minutes. A loud crash startled him and dragged his attention back to the job in hand. He looked down and was immediately disappointed, it was a mirror, one of the smaller twenties; he watched the carp in the clear water as it swam away from the island. He leaned back against the trunk and pulled a notebook from his pocket, glanced at the time on his chunky wristwatch and made an entry. He looked down again polarising the scene with the glasses as he did so. There were still six baits in the swim. The mirror had not disturbed any of them. Previous baits that he had introduced to the lake over the last few days had all been taken. He was hoping to see what was taking them. He had been here for a few hours now and nothing had so much as sniffed the cubes. He was beginning to think that the coots were taking them, although he remembered they had been round earlier and ignored them. As he watched a huge dark shape loomed out from a weed bed several yards from the bank. The dark shadow closely followed by another even larger shadow. Saul held his breath.

Two common carp moved into the shallows under the tree. Saul, who had seen many large carp in the lake, was in awe. Both fish were copper in colour and broader than his head. The smaller of the two paused over one of the baits. There was a soft puff of disturbance on the lake bed. A tense knot of excitement formed in Saul's stomach. The fish moved on to the next bait, only when the first carp had taken two of the baits did the largest carp move forward to sample one of the four remaining free offerings. Slowly, Saul reached to his pocket and withdrew a compact digital zoom camera. Putting his wrist through the lanyard he brought the camera to his eye. Silently he closed in on the fish.

Click.

The largest carp immediately turned tightly on the spot and shot back into the weed kicking up the bottom as it turned. The other smashed its tail on to the surface sending a surprising amount of water into the air before bolting into the weed bed creating massive disturbance.

The shallows were now completely coloured, it would take ages to settle. Saul sat back against the trunk smiling as he wiped a few drops of muddy water from the camera lens with his sleeve. He pulled out the notebook from his top pocket and made another entry. It was then that he noticed a movement in the fields beyond the house. It was a car turning on to the old track that led to the farm. As he watched, another car turned on to the track behind it. He zoomed in as much as he could with the limited camera lens; it was obvious that the cars were coming here. It must be someone coming to view the house, he thought or to look at the lake. On the other hand, it might be an invasion force from the Galactic Trade Federation.

08:43

"Are you sure it's him Brian?" Tom said, as he watched the hearse turn off in the distance.

"Who else would be driving a hearse on a farm track at nine in the morning?"

Brian was upset that they were not the first to arrive.

"I just didn't expect him to be driving a hearse, I thought he might have a, well a Ford Fiesta or something."

"He has."

"Has what; a Fiesta?"

"No, he's got a Nissan something or other."

"Why ain't he using it?"

"Tom I don't know, perhaps his wife borrowed it."

"Is he married then Bri?"

"Yes he's married."

"How long he been . . ."

Brian shot him a fierce look.

"Sorry Bri, just asking."

They turned left on to another narrow farm track and followed it down the hill toward the wood. Even from this high point in the road it was difficult to see where the lake was. They could see the gate and the short drive to a crumbling house, beyond that they could see little else other than trees and thick undergrowth. Brian followed fresh tyre marks round to the back of the house. The track led out on to a large open area surrounded by a sea of colour. The wood had swallowed up what used to be the garden. Young trees had advanced into the ragged flowerbeds and in turn the shrubs and flowers had invaded the lawn although the lawn was more like a patch of meadow. The grass was two feet high and inundated with wild flowers. Brian noticed, to his annoyance, the rear end of Collins Saab sticking out from behind the hearse. Both cars were empty and he could see no one in the garden. He pulled up next to the hearse and shut off the engine.

They looked around at the overgrown scene. A million insects going about their business greeted Tom as he slid open the window. The slow breeze carried the heady scents of thousands of overgrown flowers into the Landrover. Brian opened his door and stepped out into the soft damp grass. It was so peaceful that he did not want to slam the door so he just pushed it too.

He took a few steps and stood with his eyes closed feeling the morning sun. Tom was next to him taking a deep breath, the wet mud on his clothes starting to steam.

"This is fantastic Bri, can you believe this place?"

They turned and looked back at the house, it was practically a ruin. Built of natural materials it was obviously very old. Some of the brick coins had toppled taking the flint infill with them exposing the interior. The roof had collapsed at one end the rest leaning heavily on the chimney stack. Most of the terracotta tiles had slipped from the timbers leaving only the skeletal remains; every surface was covered with greenery. It seemed that every plant in the woodland had claimed a stake on this property. It was as if the wood were absorbing the house, another ten years and you might never see it again. The lazy scene had calmed Brian considerably.

"It's all a bit knackered Tom. I wonder what the new owners will do with it."

A voice directly behind them made them both jump.

"They are going to pull it down."

Brian and Tom spun round to find Russell standing there smiling.

"My uncle has been instructed to make it safe, maybe pull it down. Collin's here, he's walking down to the lake, there's a path through the trees." He looked down at Brian's feet and then Tom's sodden clothes. "I think that you're taking the idea of camouflage a bit too far, don't you?"

08:49

Saul decided to wait on the island until the intruders had gone; there was no point in giving away his position. He scrambled, half slid down the lightning tree and grabbed his rucksack. He crawled through the bushes to the other side of the island, to a short grassy section of bank. Saul untied a small raft, cursing himself for disturbing the coots. As they ran noisily across the water, Saul imagined the visitors pointing and shouting, sending troops around the bank to investigate. Beneath the over hanging bushes he secured the raft out of sight. Quickly he manoeuvred himself through the shrubs to a position where he could observe the intruders unseen. He pushed a few stems out of the way and employed the binoculars just in time to see a man arrive at the lakeside. He was dressed in a modern camouflage shirt, topped with a camouflage baseball cap. From the way he was looking around it seemed to be the lake he was interested in. Saul watched him through the lens he felt like a sniper, he felt safe at this distance.

09:08

They walked down a wide overgrown track through the wood. As they neared the lake, the trees became much closer, older. Thick trunks sprouted twisted boughs heavy with leaf. The leaves were small and stunted, useless in the low light conditions. Only the leaves at the crown were fully developed, basking in the glorious summer above. The sounds of their footsteps were absorbed by the soft leaf-strewn ground, down the hill they walked in cool silence.

The air had become damp Tom felt a chill though his wet muddy clothes, the track had turned into a tunnel, no more sun reached the three men. The only light was the sun reflecting off the water ahead appearing as a dazzling pyrotechnic display at the end of the tunnel. The tunnel had narrowed to an exit about the size of a garage door they stepped through and out of the gloom shielding their eyes from the glare.

Two things hit their senses at the same time. The noise, in contrast with the tunnel the sound was deafening. Tom was so shocked that he took a few steps back. He shook his head as he emerged again.

"Wow," he breathed.

Then there was the air; it was thick, hot and humid, like stepping from an air-conditioned plane into a South American rain forest. Tom's breathing sounded laboured while his lungs adjusted to the new atmosphere.

The thick woods rose up with the landscape all around the water creating a huge natural amphitheatre. Life was concentrated around the water source, robins, finches, thrushes, wood pigeons wood peckers, crickets, bees, dragonflies, mice moths midges and quite possibly pterodactyls.

Ten human ears tuned into a loud crash that came from the far side of the lake, then another. Fish sucking insects from the top continually broke the lake surface. A deep set of bow waves carved their way along the front of the expansive reed bed.

Collin was just ahead, standing with one foot up on a post, the remains of a small derelict jetty. He was lost in the ambience he barely acknowledged them as Brian Tom and Russell stood by his side silently facing the lake.

They watched swallows swoop down to the water's surface, twisting and turning in the pursuit of breakfast. He had never seen so much life in one place. Thousands of species, flora and fauna were interacting, communicating, playing out determined roles in the ecosystem. It was beautiful; Collin saw it like a machine, like intricate clockwork with everything happening at once, each part relying on all the others. Here, it was obvious how it all fitted together. He tried to think of something man made that displayed the same perfection, but nothing would come to mind.

Brian laid a gentle hand on his shoulder and whispered in his ear.

"We are going to kick the arse out of this lake."

Saul's eyes widened when he saw another three people join the first man at the lakeside. They were all dressed in either green or camouflage clothing. For some reason the shortest man seemed to be caked in mud. He focused in on the tall man.

Saul immediately pulled back from the edge, lowering the binoculars his heart increased its pace. Suddenly he did not feel so secure.

Collin had latched on to Russell, prizing information about depths and weed banks from his seemingly endless knowledge of the lake. Brian walked with Tom just behind. All were pointing and discussing features and potential swims. About a third of the way round they came to a wide stream, an overflow for the lake.

Russell explained that the lake was natural, created around an underground spring. The stream was very wide and deep as it left the lake. They walked down about fifty yards and the stream started to narrow. When the stream was only twenty feet across, Russell stopped.

"Watch," he said, then he stepped out from the bank grinning. He appeared to walk on the water.

Russell was laughing from the other side of the stream his feet hardly wet. Tom stooped to look at the water through his Polaroids and in the dappled sunlight he could make out five stepping stones just under the surface. He ran across the water laughing to join Russell. Brian watched Collin take a sedate stroll on the stream before taking his own first hesitant step. Holding out his arms to balance himself he took the journey one stone at a time, ignoring the derisory comments from his friends. On the third stone, he stopped to adjust his balance extending his arms a little more, like a tightrope walker. He stood with both feet together trying to get purchase on the stone. A soft beam of sunlight broke through the foliage illuminating the worried look on Brian's unshaven face.

"Come on mate, you look like bloody Jesus. Sort it out," Tom said giggling. "I'm surprised you even bothered with the stepping stones."

Brian shook with laughter, the movement too much for his sense of balance. He slipped off the stone and plunged thigh deep in cold water.

Saul could hear the splash and the laughter although he dare not look. The island was quite close to the stream. He would wait until he heard them move round the bank a little before he risked further surveillance. He watched them until they came to the reed bed.

09:56

Russell stopped and turned to the others.

"There is a way through the reeds, but it's pretty dangerous if you don't know the path. So always go around, it takes a lot longer, but trust me you don't want to get lost in there." Russell jerked a thumb over to his right indicating the reed bed. Tom thought that he caught an odd look in Russell's eyes.

They all followed Russell around the Reeds. Even at the edge it was obvious that he was picking out a specific path. The trees came right down to the lake. The landscape went seamlessly from thick wood to thick reeds. The area that they were picking their way through was more like the everglades than rural England. Huge swarms of insects clouded around them. Where the sun found its way to the water Brian could see hundreds of small fry darting between the reeds and hundreds more midges drying their wings before joining the clouds above them. He could hear Collin cursing and a slap or two from Tom. He looked up and was not at all surprised to notice that not one single insect was flying anywhere near Russell. There just seemed to be a hole in the cloud wherever Russell was standing. Brian brushed a hand through his hair to dislodge a layer of hitchhikers and caught up with Russell. He stayed as close to him as he could till they came back to the open stretch of bank leading back to the tunnel from where they had started.

Brian was relieved and a little annoyed to discover that there was in fact a small bridge further down the stream. What Russell called a bridge was in fact a few thick planks set just above a weir stretching across the stream. The planks were old and twisted no evidence of a handrail or rope, nothing to suggest a safe crossing. As they walked across, the planks would dip and bounce alarmingly, soaking the pedestrian's feet.

They managed to reverse the cars, one at a time, down the track to unload. All the tackle was brought over the stream by hand or by barrow clockwise around the lake. Russell helped everyone carry something, his own tackle comprised of one rod, net and a light bag. This lack of equipment completely dumbfounded Collin; he pushed an overloaded barrow along by Russell's side.

"You have to be prepared for anything," he said. "Distance, margin, spod, method. You never know what it will take to catch the carp you want." He slowed to bump the wheel over one of the many thick tree roots that dissected the track. "And I like my comforts, if you're going to sit somewhere for a few days you've got be comfortable."

11:14

Saul was now regretting his decision to stay on the island. He wanted to surprise Russell, but he knew that as soon as he found out that he was there, he would stand little chance of sneaking up on him. Russell and the man with the big barrow had stopped fifty yards past the stream where the bank was still close to the island. The other two had carried on around to the opposite side and stopped ten yards or so from the start of the reed bed.

Saul could not observe everyone at the same time without giving away his position to at least one of the parties. He crawled through the long grass to watch the reed swim. He put the binoculars to his eyes then slowly peered around the base of the tree, one of the men was pointing right at him. The magnified image made him jump he resisted the urge to move forcing himself to become motionless. He knew that all predators' eyes have evolved to notice quick movements and man was a predator. The angler was pointing at the swim beneath the tree directly in front of him and he was saying something to the other person. Saul waited until they had turned their heads then he slipped back behind the trunk.

The sun was getting higher and Saul was trying to decide what to do. The swish of a casting rod interrupted this process so he peered around the tree to see where the lead would land. As he did so there was a whistling sound instantly followed by a two-ounce lead thudding into the tree inches from his face. Saul flinched back and swore. He clamped a hand over his mouth his eyes open wide. He could hear laughing from the bank sixty or so yards away. Slowly he moved his hand from his mouth, listening intently to the voices carried across on the still air, not daring to breath.

"Bloody hell Bri I think you just hit a duck, I swear I see something move just then." Tom was shielding his eyes from the sun's glare and laughing. "There's one very angry duck out there Bri, watch yourself mate."

Brian was pulling the lead back to reset the line clip, he could not see much in the glare.

"Is there Tom, did I hit a duck?" He looked at Tom who was laughing. "You're winding me up you git. Pass me those glasses mate I can't see bugger all here."

Tom grabbed Brian's sunglasses and pulled his own from his top pocket.

They both placed a rod out to the island. Tom put his second rod along the bank toward the reeds on his left and Brian cast his right rod to a set of lilies twenty yards out. Brian finished setting the last indicator and joined Tom on the chairs, Tom handed him a cold beer. Brian patted his top pocket.

"Sod it! I've left my fags in the car."

Saul's heart had slowed down, in the last hour he had heard four rods go in, two were only yards from where he lay. He had watched Brian use a spod rod to bait his close in swim with some sort of particle mix. He could not help himself being intrigued about what bait they were using. Slithering through the island undergrowth Saul made his way over to watch the stream. He looked back just in time to see one of the two men start to make his way back round the lake. Saul moved to a different spot to get a better view. It was the guy who had made the offensive cast.

Brian walked along the bank chewing a stem of grass, as he past an old tree stump something caught his eye. Brian was a bit surprised to say the least. A tiny figure was peeking out from the thick grass at the base of the rotting stump. He smiled to himself turning it over in his hands. Definitely a childhood memory, he thought, not his childhood though. This must belong to Russell he must have dropped it all those years ago when poaching the lake. Brian put the figure into his shirt pocket there was only one thing to do. He was sure that Russell would enjoy the memories attached to the figure, but not before Brian had teased him about it.

Saul lowered the binoculars, his eyes blazed his breathing became more rapid. It was bad enough that they had invaded his lands and then fired on his position, narrowly avoiding injury. Now they had kidnapped the Princess. Saul slithered over to the other swim, a short observation revealed tackle man fussing about setting up a bivvy, Russell was brewing up on a small stove. Saul watched as the kidnapper stopped briefly to talk to Russell. This is it, thought Saul, as soon as he shows Russell the princess, Russell would be curious and then suspicious. He pressed the binoculars harder into his eyes, tense and nervous. The kidnapper did not touch his top pocket he did not seem to mention his find. Saul watched him walk back to the house and the cars. Fifteen minutes later he returned smoking a cigarette. He did not stop with Russell, but continued on back to his rods. Saul slowly backed away from his position until totally hidden in the shaded centre of the island. He took stock of his rucksack, some cheese sandwiches and a flask of drink, two magazines, bag of crisps, lightweight jacket and a 35 mm camera that carried a decent sized zoom lens, everything had been packed into plastic bags.

Satisfied that he would be comfortable for the rest of the day he rolled up the jacket and used it to sit on. After all, there was little to do but wait, maybe a few sniper shots with the zoom later, although he never counted sniper shots as proof of capture. He took off his bulky wristwatch and slipped it into the side pocket of the rucksack. Plenty of time before he had to get back, he pulled out an old copy of Soldier of Fortune, opened the first page, but changed his mind. He returned it to the rucksack and pulled out the latest Combat and Survival. He lay back on the ground using the jacket as a pillow, occasionally having to stifle his laughter.

12:26

C ollin sipped the tea and tightened his grip on the branch.

"Are you ok there Collin," Russell said from above him. "You could climb higher up next to me, there's plenty of room."

"No, this is fine, this is high enough. I can see the hole in the weed that you were talking about and the shallows by the island look interesting." He gestured with his cup toward the island. The branch that he was standing on swayed; he tightened his grip a little more.

"You can forget the island until dusk," Russell said. "Keep to the deeper water or on the top."

As if on cue a large mirror broke the surface, turned over in a slow fat lazy way and disappeared into the depths.

"Nice," Collin said. "How about you Russ, where are you setting up?"

Looking up he realised that Russell had gone. He looked down and Russell was on the ground looking back with a smile. Collin made a clumsy decent to join him, Russell had started to assemble his rod. Collin took a second look, for some reason he had been expecting something a bit more Chris Yates, maybe an old split cane rod and centre pin reel. Far from it, the rod was a beautiful Greys X-Flite coupled with a Shimano 10,000. Collin watched Russell tie a small barb-less hook to the line and that seemed to be it. Collin walked to his own rods on their pod, baited and ready to cast.

"I will have to find that hole with the marker rod."

Russell walked to the edge of the water and picked up a small stone, after a moments thought he tossed the stone in.

"There you go Cole' just there."

Collin was going to ask if Russell was sure, but thought better of it. He dutifully dropped his left rod on to the spot, sank the line and set the indicator.

"Where do you think the other one should go?"

Russell had disappeared again.

Fifty yards down the bank Russell was up to his waist in warm water on the edge of some light reeds. He was sitting on a sunken tree trunk waiting. A light mesh net draped over him concealed his outline, his rod held up in the air, like a crafty gnome he waited. Russell watched a single grain of maize nicked on to the hook as it swung gently a few inches from the water's surface. He listened to a crash in the reeds behind him which made him do nothing, the reeds a few feet away from him were disturbed from beneath, Russell did nothing. A mirror of some considerable size rolled directly in front of him, less than six feet away. Nothing: he waited and listened. Ten minutes later a crash in the reeds behind him made him gently lower the rod so that the maize was touching the water. He noticed the reeds move next to him, he released the bail arm. The maize sank slowly into the water. He closed the arm as soon as he saw the loose line start to pull away. A millisecond later the rod tip ripped down with massive force.

Collin relaxed in the chair, rods out bivvy set, time for a beer. He pulled a can from the cool box. There had been a crashing sound from down the bank a short while ago, in a petty way he hoped that it was Russell falling in. More realistically, he thought that Russell would come back with a twenty pounder under each arm, having caught them using only his hat.

Twenty five minutes later a voice behind him made him jump.

"I just had a super mirror down by the stream."

He turned round slowly trying not to look surprised, Russell was crouching next to his chair holding out an expensive digital camera. Collin wiped some spilt beer from his chin and then looked at the display screen. It was indeed a fantastic fish, fully scaled, rich in colour.

"Beautiful," he said. "What's it weigh?"

"Twenty four."

"Lovely, are they all like this in here?"

"Judging by the shape and colour it is one of the original strains. I doubt that it has ever been restocked. It's a very old lake I was catching carp over twenty when I was in my teens. I have records of fish looking exactly . . ."

Russell tapped Collin lightly on the knee and pointed at the tip of Collin's left rod. They watched the tip tremble in an odd fashion. The tip tore violently round to the left the indicator slamming to the top, the buzzer screaming a continuous tone. Collin was on it. Russell laughed as he watched the beer can roll down the bank after Collin. The buzzer stopped and Collin was into the fish.

"Hole in the weed, pva bag," he glanced briefly back to Russell smiling. "Thanks Russ, this feels big."

The fish was pulling slow and heavy in the deep water. Russell was next to Collin now telling him to avoid a potential snag. Collin took more control and steered the fish back toward him. After ten heart pounding minutes he had it in front of him and allowed Russell to land it. The fish only weighed fifteen pounds, stunning to look at, slim and fit, but only fifteen pounds. Collin would have sworn that the carp had fought like a mid twenty. He released the mirror with a bit more respect than when he hooked it. If that was only a fifteen what did a twenty four fight like? He had a little more respect for Russell.

13:34

" **L** ila."

"Leia."

"What?"

"It's princes Leia, not Lila, Just give it back to him," Tom said tossing the figure back to Brian.

"Ah come on, It would crack me up if we could get this on the end of his line."

"Not a chance mate too many fish queuing up. Nah, give it back," Tom said chuckling.

"I'll think of something," Brian said and returned the princess to her pocket prison. "Don't tell him though. I wonder how they are getting on."

Beep Beep.

Brian was half out of the chair before he realised that it was his mobile.

"It's a text from Collin it says 'both had one Russ on way round'. He's sent a picture of his one." Brian leaned across to show Tom.

Tom leapt from his chair moving quickly toward his rods, one of which was straining silently on its rest. He snatched up the rod, no need to strike. The rod bent along its full length as Tom tried to steer the fish away from the thick reeds on his left.

"Bloody hell Bri it's like a train it's going round the front of the reeds, I forgot to turn the bloody buzzer on. I just see the rod pull round. Damm, I'm going to have to go in mate."

Tom stepped into the shallow water and started to wade out. The bottom was firm and stony so Tom felt quite comfortable up to his ribs in the water. Now in line with the front of the reeds Tom could exert some more positive control over the situation. He managed to recover a few yards of line and stop the fish heading down the first of the deep channels that led into the reeds. The carp kited off to the right away from the reeds, the sudden change in direction causing the line to slacken alarmingly. Tom spun the reel handle furiously trying to keep up. The fish tore off again, despite hooking the fish at twenty yards it was now fifty yards from the bank and had moved into some very deep water. Tom glanced over his shoulder where Brian, rather optimistically, was in the water behind him with the net. The fish slowed in the deep water Tom breathed a sigh of relief convinced that he was exerting some sort of control over the situation. Then everything ground to a halt, it was a stand off, neither Tom or fish were moving.

Guided by Brian, Tom worked his way to the bank, gently back winding as he did so. Brian steadied him as he stepped backwards on to the dry land. The line was tight, unmoving, Tom was the first to speak.

"It's not moving it might have snagged me. Bloody hell though mate, did you see how fast it moved away from those reeds. Christ!"

His rod tip slammed down again and the clutch screamed. The carp tore off to the right again, buzzers started to sound as the fish dragged through the lines of the two island rods.

Brian was trying to figure out how to get out of the cross line situation and swearing loudly. Tom had now walked down the bank to the right. He leaned back as Brian passed rods underneath him then over his head. Free of the other lines Tom felt a bit more confident. The carp was steadily heading for the patch of lilies. Brian was already reeling in his other rod to give Tom all the room he needed.

"If it reaches those lilies I'm in trub', but I can't stop it," he applied a few more ounces of pressure. "Ahh nuts!"

Tom stumbled backwards, the line now completely slack. The fish was free. Tom retrieved the limp line shaking his head. They were surprised to find everything intact minus the lead. Tom studied the hook length; it was perfect, complete with pellet on the short hair. They looked around at the devastation. All four rods were out of the water, the two middle rods still tangled together. They were both soaking wet and Tom had lost what felt like the biggest fish he had ever hooked.

Russell walked up to find them in fits of laughter. He looked them up and down.

"I see you've managed to wash the mud off."

Russell brewed up while the others re-set and changed clothes. Tom strung up a line and they hung the wet clothes in the sun and sat down for a drink. Brian had hardly finished stirring his coffee when his right rod was away.

"It's only been in ten minutes," he laughed as he struck into the fish. "It's not that big, but he's quick."

Tom's left indicator started to rise, the alarm emitting slow individual bleeps. Brian looked over his shoulder.

"It's not me mate."

Tom was over the rod. The line was being pulled away very slowly, he picked up the rod not striking, but feeling for any resistance. The gentle pull continued. He looked over at Russell who nodded and Tom struck.

Brian was in the process of landing a small double figure, he glanced round to see Tom's rod bend double his line tearing through the water away to his left again. Five seconds later it came springing back wrapping itself round the rod tip.

"I don't believe it I just don't bloody believe it," Tom shouted in frustration. "Two fish in two casts."

This time the line had snapped. Russell took a photo for Brian while Tom stomped to his bivvy muttering about running out of leads at this rate. Brian's left rod tore off as he was returning the first fish. He leapt to it, but struck into nothing.

14:40

Tom was discussing tackle with Russell.

"It's the age old problem the more you step up the tackle to cater for bigger fish the less chance one of them will take the bait."

"I disagree Tom, I think it's about the way you use the tackle. Keep it as simple as possible. The strongest chain has the fewest links."

"That is very true and fine if you're fishing six feet out or hiding in a reed bed or tree, but if you're fishing a gravel pit and have to cast ninety yards to a bar, your chain has to have more links."

"Why would you want to fish at ninety yards?"

"Because that's where the big fish are."

"True Tom that is where some big fish are some of the time. The rest of the time they must be somewhere else."

"But I have hooked two huge fish," Tom countered.

"Yes and lost two huge fish, because of the links in your chain and the distance you hooked them at."

Brian was drying his hands before attaching a pva bag.

"You're wasting your time Tom. You won't change his opinion. In fact, he will talk you round. You will go home sell all your kit bar one rod and start sticking leaves in your hat."

He grinned at Russell.

16:45

Saul was very happy because he had managed to capture the look of total disappointment on the little guys face as the fish snapped him up the second time. The zoom lens was providing plenty of entertainment, but he was intrigued by the two fish that the little guy had lost. Saul suspected one or both of the two big commons that he had seen first thing that morning. That seemed like an age ago, still there was plenty of time to plan the reprisals.

He retreated to the centre for a spot of lunch. A repeated heavy splashing told him that Tackle man was spodding toward the island. Saul had never tried large areas of bait so he was curious to see what would happen. He also decided that he did not like too much splashing on his lake and that Tackle man would be the first target. No time for elaborate traps, he will have to go on the offensive.

18:05

Through the afternoon Tom broke his duck with a string of two upper doubles and a twenty. Brian had two superb mirrors; one at eighteen and another at twenty five. Collin had steadily netted eight carp in the as many hours all around the ten pound mark. He had celebrated every one with a can of beer. He fumbled through his pockets and found his mobile and read the text. He reeled in the rods. After securing everything in the bivvy, he made his way around the lake to meet Brian and Tom.

"Hi guys, where's Russ?"

"Behind you," Tom said, pointing with a wooden spoon.

Sure enough Russell appeared by Collin's side. Tom finished off the stew and dished it up. Twenty minutes of silent chewing was followed by the scraping of spoons on plastic plates.

"Handsome," Collin said.

"Excellent Tom, that was the nuts," Brian said, he got up and collected the plates. The kettle went on and the cigarettes came out, they relaxed in the evening sun.

"So let's have the catches so far then," Tom said pulling out a scrap of paper and a short pencil. He noted all the day's fish and so far Brian had the largest with a twenty five pound Mirror. Tom looked up and noticed the weather front appearing on the distant tree line.

"Wow, look at that cloud over on the other side," he pointed across the water. "Can you feel any wind? It's starting to move the water over there. We could be in for a wet night. Blimey Russ, what do you do in the rain? You're welcome to duck into my bivvy if it gets too bad."

"Thanks all the same Tom, but I've got a shelter in the bag there and a bed."

Everyone looked at the small bag in disbelief.

"You are right about the wet night though and the water is moving on the other side." Russell watched the pattern on the water a little longer. "Is your gear all right over the other side Cole?"

"Yeah, I threw everything in the Viper, rock solid."

Food, hot food, Saul could smell it. He opened his eyes half expecting to be at home. He grinned and shuffled over to observe the reed swim now positively identified as the source of the smell. The little man was handing out plates of food and food took time to eat, everyone had sat down. Saul made a snap decision, he moved fast to the other side of the island snatching up his rucksack and jacket he made for the raft. Fumbling with the knot seemed to take ages. With the rucksack, his trainers, jacket and shirt on the raft, he slid into the water and started to swim for the stream. Half way across he realised that he was causing some deep ripples on the water that could give him away. Too late now, despite knowing that he would be hidden behind the island, he felt very exposed. A sudden forceful gusty wind hit the lake covering some of his tracks, but it pushed him off course making it harder to swim with the raft in tow. He made it to the stream and headed for the bank. He pulled the raft along the edge until he came to a clear spot. Here he dragged the raft from the water and concealed it under some brambles growing at the side of the track.

He ran back to the lake using the binoculars to observe any reaction from the enemy camp. Nothing: still eating what Saul considered to be their last supper. He moved to within a few meters of Collins bivvy, any further and he would be visible from the other bank. He studied the water line; thick weed disguised the true depth at the edge. The grass was short and tufty, no real cover there, maybe the tree? He could lure him to the rods easy enough, he thought. Yes, lure him out of the bivvy. He looked up, the strong wind had delivered a thick blanket of low cloud which was moving over the lake, Saul could feel the pressure dropping, he headed for the den.

"What's the plan then Russ?" Brian said, idly pointing at the Thick lid of cloud that was slowly settling above the lake.

A deep shadow engulfed them the cloud denied the sun any further access. As one man Tom Russell and Brian took off their sunglasses. Collin pulled a bottle of JD from inside his jacket, took a long swig then passed it on. Russell took a quick sip and did the same.

"I'm going to bivvy up over by Cole I saw the perfect spot earlier. Then I'm going to catch me a common," Russell said.

Once the top was back on the bottle Russell and Collin made their way round to the viper. Collin set about fitting an extreme winter skin to the titan, Russell gave him a hand then left him to peg it out while he set up his own sleeping arrangements.

"You're not going to sleep on that."

Collin gestured toward the delicate looking hammock strung beneath a mozzy net and rain cover. The wind was pushing the hammock back and forth.

"Brian wasn't kidding when he said that you would give Bear Grylls a run for his money."

Russell finished hanging his kit under the tarp.

"I'm going round to catch a common."

Collin watched him slide into the trees. He called out after him.

"You didn't say how big."

Russell's voice floated back on the wind.

"Twenty two pounds."

Collin recast and stood by the rods wondering why it was so dark. The wind was tugging at his clothes. He pulled off the sunglasses, it made little difference, the lid of cloud had now closed. The wind that had brought the cloud suddenly dropped away to nothing. He could smell the flowers from the garden, the scent left hanging in the thickening air. All sounds seemed muffled, like events in the next room or surround sound with the treble turned down. Within minutes a dense mist started to form on the water. He took a long pull on the bottle, the pressure dropped a little more and the temperature started to go up.

20:22

One two three four five, despite the failing light Russell skipped across the stepping stones and on to the far bank with practised ease. Around the lake to the edge of the reeds, he did not hesitate he just waded into the lake walking straight out from the bank. At ten yards he was up to his chest in the warm water. He carried on walking parallel to the reeds, landing net and rod held above his head. Another ten yards and the water started to shallow, Russell was soon kneeling on the bottom of the lake, the calm water coming up to his waist.

The wind had dropped to nothing the only ripples were his. He was fifty yards from the bank where he had started, but was now only three or four yards from the front of the deep reed bed.

Russell tethered his landing net to his wrist and allowed it to float behind him on a length of cord. He could not see Brian and Tom's bivvies in the distance on the far side of the reeds, but he could tell that they were down at the water's edge. Russell could not make out who was landing a fish only the headlamps cutting through the rising mist. A few minutes later he saw the flash of a camera, must be a decent carp he thought, but concluded that the fight was far too short to be one of the fish he was stalking, he resumed his watch.

The last of the light dissolved into the heavy air, the mist was soaking into Russell's hat. There were moments when Russell could not see anything at all.

Another flash from the other end of the reeds and he could hear laughter from Tom and Brian on the distant bank. He tuned it out focussing on the reeds he could barely see. Just then he noticed one of the thick stems moving from side to side, Russell knew from experience that a large carp was nudging the reed out of the way. He listened for the sucking sound he knew the carp would make as it fed on the surface. Topping fish, some only yards behind him, made it difficult to pinpoint sounds directly ahead. A bat swooped close enough for Russell to feel the temporary wind from its wings, he flinched his head back and heard a new noise to his left, but oddly above him.

He looked and immediately threw himself flat to the water spooking a large common just beneath the surface. The huge swan missed him by inches and landed heavily carving a deep groove in the calm water. Russell surfaced treading and spitting out water, he scrambled back to his shallow perch. He watched the mist roll in to cover the flight path. The swan's ghostly shape, oblivious to Russell, moved silently into a gap in the reeds. Russell shook his head and made his way back to the bank.

No chance of success tonight, he moved around the back of the reeds to see what Tom and Brian had been catching.

21:48

Saul crept along the edge of the bank slowly parting his way through the blanket weed. The mist was troubling Saul, he would have preferred clear air for the shot. Using the flash unit in the mist could cause a white out. He risked a peek over the edge, all was quiet and he could just make out the outline of the bivvy although there were no lights. He thought of Russell, not the only one up to his neck in water tonight, he suppressed a laugh. Saul knew about the shallow spot on the edge of the reeds. He had nearly walked into Russell on the track when he had returned from the den. He had watched Russell, when the mist allowed, for over an hour before the swan arrived. He almost shouted out to warn his cousin, but was now glad that he had not.

He reached the spot beneath his targets rod tips and rested quietly in the dark. He rubbed his hands together drying his fingers. He hoped that tackle man did not get a real run in the next few minutes. He reached up to the small camera strapped to his forehead and removed the lens cap.

A tiny river of Jack Daniels was trickling its way down Collin's t-shirt evaporating as it soaked into the fabric. Slowly, deliberately without opening his eyes Collin fumbled for the bottle top and replaced it.

He was so thirsty, tea, a cup of tea, he thought. He swung his legs down off the bed chair and sat up. The bottle thumped to the floor Collin flicked on the headlamp. The bottle was fine; he took a couple of deep breaths and checked the extent of the leakage on his t-shirt.

His body lurched forward the second he heard the buzzer, half way to the rods he started to slide on the damp grass. Surprised at his own grace he slid like a surfer the rest of the way to the rods laughing out loud. He struck into nothing the line completely slack, there was a big crash in front of him, he peered down. A dark shape rose up from the water.

Click.

A stunning white light knocked him backwards, Collin stumbled into his pod setting the buzzers off. Blindly trying to free himself he lost his balance and pitched forwards dragging the pod with him into the water.

Saul's mouth dropped open as Collin sailed passed tangled in the pod, he ducked as the butt of a rod flew over narrowly missing his head. He watched the lights on the buzzers sink into the water. He clambered up the bank, clear of the water he was about to leave when he realised that his victim had not surfaced.

He ripped the camera from his head and plunged back in. Quickly he found the weed covered spluttering Collin and dragged him to the edge. He tried to pull his victim from the water, but only managed to get him half out.

Collin was cursing now and starting to drag himself from the lake, Saul backed off satisfied that he would be ok.

A beeping ring tone from the bivvy and a bright flash above his head make Saul jump, for a second he thought that someone had taken his picture. Then he felt, rather than heard, the start of the thunder, a deep rolling that shook the condensing mist from the trees and echoed around the landscape. The air moved; all the mist was being sucked in toward the island, like the tide going out before a tsunami. The mist rose like a column over the island up into the low clouds. A silent pause before wind and rain came flooding back. The first gust nearly took Saul off his feet, the horizontal rain stung his face and hands.

The storm settled on the lake.

"Collin's had one by the looks of it I just see the flash," Tom said.

They all heard the distant crash as Collin went in. Brian reached for his mobile.

"What is he doing over there?" he rang Collins number. "Jesus did you see that lightning. Sod it I've lost the signal."

"Look at the mist," Tom said, standing up and pointing.

The storm settled on the lake.

21:55

Collin thought that he must be dead and was now in some sort of muddy wet heaven. He crawled toward the bivvy on his hands and knees, once inside he collapsed into his bed chair his hand landing on the bottle. Rolling over he took a long glug of whisky and passed out, a small river of Jack Daniels ran down his shirt.

With help from Russell, they franticly stowed all the gear away into the bivvies out of the driving rain, Brian tried the mobile again.

"No answer," he said. "Come on Russ' lets get over there."

Brian and Russell made their way round to Collin. The rain was intense, their light clothing offered no protection, by the time they arrived at Collin's bivvy they were soaked through to the skin.

"Where are the rods?" Russell said.

Brian went straight to the bivvy, Russell to where the rods should have been.

"He's here," Brian said. "He's in here, he's a mess, he's been in the lake all right and he stinks of booze. We can't leave him here everything is soaked. Russ . . . RUSS."

Russell had retrieved the rods and the pod, he crouched in the bivvy doorway.

"Your right Bri, lets get him up to the house, I have some dry clothes in the back of the car."

They zipped up the bivvy and carried Collin slumped between them around the lake and toward the house. Russell waded across the stream, easily carrying Colin's limp body across his shoulder; Brian was surprised at Russell's strength.

Saul was now moving in the opposite direction toward Tom, or target two, as Saul had named him. The wind was constant, driving the rain at a steady forty-five degrees and gusting to horizontal. As he moved round he noticed that there was no calm side to the water. The wind was swirling round the lake like a tornado.

22:48

" **T**he light, the light," Collin muttered.

"What's he on about Russ?" Brian said. "What happened?"

Russell opened the tailgate. They dried Collin off as best they could and stripped him down to his shorts. They managed to get him into a set of overalls that Russell kept in the car for breakdowns. The overalls swamped Collin. Once in the back Collin crawled further into the hearse passed out and started to snore loudly. Russell draped the old blanket over Collin's unconscious body. They watched him for a minute until satisfied that he would be ok.

Russell and Brian made their way back to the lake, as they picked their way around the bank heading for Tom they saw a flash from the bivvies. A quick glance between them and they started to run. They stumbled along the track, Brian staying close to Russell as he navigated the edge of the reeds. They rushed up to Tom who was standing at the waters edge.

"Ah, just in time Bri," Tom said. "Land this for me will you mate, hi Russ, how's Collin Did he have another fish?"

Over the weighing, they told Tom about Collin.

"So what actually happened then?" Tom asked. "Did he fall in or what?"

"Who knows," Brian answered. "He was drunk that's for sure and he had definitely been in. He kept saying something about a light, kept mumbling on about it. So when we saw the flash from here we thought, well I thought; oh, I don't know."

Tom was laughing as he picked up the fish and waded into the shallows to release it by the reeds.

"The flash was just me fiddling with the camera, nearly blinded myself. That's when I got the run, how funny's that." He laid the fish in the water holding it gently as it recovered. He looked back and shouted over his shoulder above the rain. "Bri . . . BRIAN. Could you make sure I put that Camera back in the case, I don't want it to get damp." He looked down something had made the carp bolt from his fingertips with a splash.

Click.

Tom leaped backwards, arms across his face landing flat on his back thrashing about in the water. Russell and Brian crashed into the shallows to help their friend.

The commotion allowed Saul to retreat into the reeds. Two down two to go. His cover was blown this was no longer a covert operation. He could hear the shouts fading behind him. Sliding himself between thick reeds he made his way to the bank then he headed for the den.

Then something caught up with him, cutting through the rain, riding above the rumbling sky. One word entered his ear, clear and audible as if the speaker were inches from his head, one word.

"Damm it," Brian swore as they dragged Tom to the edge. "What's going on? . . . Russ . . . Russell."

"There seems to be someone else on the lake Bri."

"No shit Sherlock; who else is on the lake?"

Tom sat up, dragged the hat from his head and slammed it to the muddy ground.

"I am running out of bloody clothes," he shouted and spat out a sprig of weed. He started to wring out the hem of his jersey. "I saw a bloke, in the bloody reeds. I looked round and he just appeared I threw my hands up just as the flash went off so I got off light, so to speak."

"Do you know who it is Russ?" Brian said.

They both looked at Russell. Russell nodded and stood looking out over the water. He took a deep breath and shouted.

"SAUL."

Tom and Brian were stunned, there was a long pause.

"Bloody hell Russ that was a bit loud."

Tom agreed to stay with the bivvies while Russell and Brian went in search of Saul.

"Some family you got Russ, are you sure it's your cousin and not some bleeding escaped nutter?" Brian said.

"I'm sure Bri. I thought I saw something earlier while we were eating, just before the cloud came over, when Tom noticed the wind on the far side. I think that was Saul leaving the island. He must have been on there all day, but don't ask me why. We may have upset him somehow."

"Upset him, too right I'm going to upset him."

Russell said no more, but quickened his pace pressing on through the last of the reeds. They headed around the track back toward Collin's bivvy.

"Hang on Russ I need to have a jimmy," Brian said, he stepped to the side of the track and started to relieve himself.

Russell waited taking the opportunity to look around and get his bearings. Everything was black, he could barely see Brian who was only a few yards away; he would have to rely on his mental map of the lake.

"Blimey! Take extra care along here Russ, there's a bit of a slope down the side of this track," Brian said. He zipped up and took the torch out of his mouth, shining the beam down. "Christ, it's practically a shear drop here," he said stepping back from the edge.

Russell loomed up next to him and looked down.

"Come on Bri, this is not a new feature, there must be something down there."

They scrambled down a gentler slope twenty yards further down the track and then made their way back through the trees. It was obvious that many years ago a very large tree had fallen away from the edge of the track leaving a large hole in the bank. Some one had cleared the area. There was a kind of structure here, a sheet of woven branches and leaves, Brian pulled it away revealing a small doorway. Someone had dug into the earth bank under the track to create a small shelter. The whole thing would have been impossible to see from above, even in broad daylight.

Brian shone his torch through the narrow doorway. Despite the small entrance, there was plenty of room inside. The ceiling was lined with an old tarpaulin and reinforced with thick boughs and old planks, it was well supported. It must have taken hours and hours to dig it out. Even though the rain was making deep puddles on the track four or five feet above, the den looked dry and snug.

"You won't believe this Russ."

The beam was showing a slim bench down one side of the dugout and a low canvas seat on the other. On the bench were a rucksack and a sandwich box. Leaning against the wall above the bench was a pin board. The board was covered with photos.

Brian moved forward to go through the door. Russell grabbed his collar and held him back.

"Wait Bri let me check it out first."

Brian shrugged the hand away.

"I know he's your cousin, but he's bang out of order, he deserves a slap, he could have killed Collin and Tom is well pissed off. If there's anything in here to tell us where he is, I'm going to find it."

"That wasn't what I meant Bri; besides Collin is ok, just drunk and a bit shocked."

It was too late Brian was already half way through the low doorway on his hands and knees, torch between his teeth.

The first flash completely disorientated Brian the torch fell from his mouth. The torch went out as it landed, but that made no difference as five blinding flashes of white light illuminated the den for another second or two.

Brian instinctively tried to back out, but blinded and in shock he became trapped in the narrow doorway. He felt Russell grab him, pulling him backwards out of the den. Brian rolled out on to his back, all he could see were brilliant bright blue spots of light before his eyes, his own private laser light show whether his eyes were open or not.

"The fucker, he fucking booby trapped the fucking door, I'm going to fucking kill him when I can fucking see him." He rubbed his eyes and shook his head. "Arse."

Russell knelt down beside him.

"You'll be ok in a minute or two," he looked around at the dark bushes and trees surrounding them, listening intently. "Saul won't stay here. If he didn't see that light show he would have heard you shouting. He will be gone now, he's pretty smart."

Russell crawled toward the den and entered it very carefully, he soon recovered the torch.

"Smart, fucking smart, he fucking blinded me Russ, smart I'll give him fucking smart fucking wanker, fuck," Brian screamed above the rain

Russell could clearly hear him from the den and could not resist a smile. A modern camping lamp stood on the bench, he turned it on. A set of six flash bulbs mounted on a short strip of wood were nailed to the edge of the bench. Using the torch he traced two red wires that led to a small motion sensor above the doorway. A second wire left the sensor and travelled across the roof to a small disposable camera secured to the ceiling with rough string. This was obviously not done spontaneously, this was an organised defence. Russell scanned the twenty or so pictures pinned to the corkboard with an assortment of drawing pins fishhooks and what looked like large rose thorns. With the exception of a few sunrises and sunsets taken from various points on the lake, the rest were of animals; startled rats, birds, a squirrel looking very surprised. The rear end of a badger was pinned next to a stunning photo of an owl plucking a mouse from an old tree stump. Russell recognised it as the stump opposite the entrance to the lake.

Some photo's had been enlarged, a picture of a huge mirror carp sucking up a what looked like some sort of square boillie, maybe a cube of bread, Russell was impressed. He took a closer look at the rucksack and sandwich box, ignoring Brian who was calling him. On the bench a small empty plastic bag caught his eye. He picked it up and sniffed it then looked at the pictures again.

"Russ, come on my visions starting to come back."

Russell heard Brian fall over again and swear loudly.

Brian was getting unsteadily back on his feet again and waving his hand in front of his face.

"Russ, come on my visions starting to come back."

"Hang on Bri."

A minute later Russell crawled backwards out of the den taking a last look he turned out the lamp.

"I am going to look for Saul, you wait here till you can see better, then make your way over to Tom. We can concentrate the search over there." He had to raise his voice against the rain crashing through the trees. Russell pushed the torch into Brian's hand. "I will go check on Collin." With that, he slipped away into the trees.

Brian stood alone and turned his head up to the sky, water splashed down on to his face.

"Fucker," he shouted aloud. He rubbed the water from his eyes and started to look for the way back to the track.

A few yards away, hugging a fallen trunk, Saul listened to Brian crash through the trees, that had been a narrow escape, he thought. He could smell his sleeve where Brian had urinated on it. He had heard Brian coming up the track, it would have been hard not to, clumping along like a drunken wookie. It was not until Brian had stopped above him did he realise that someone was with him. It could only have been Russell.

Saul had moved fast thanking his lucky stars that the lamp was already turned off. He grabbed the door and placed it across the entrance as quietly as he could. He had practised emergency protocols like this with Luke and Han Solo. At the last second he reached back into the den through a small hole in the door. It seemed to take an eternity to find the switch on the battery pack, his heart was thumping. He had but a few seconds left to disappear before Brian stormed the clearing wielding the torch like a light sabre in the rain.

Saul lay there with his cheek pressed against the bark, still as a fallen statue. Any second now, he kept saying to himself, any second now the lights will shine on me. Despite the tension, he had to stifle a laugh when the first flash went off. Even though he was facing the other way with his eyes half closed against the rain he could clearly see the light from the flashes revealing the surrounding trees and quite possibly himself. The tension increased, he dare not turn his head to watch, he was far too close to move. Saul listened intently and was a little relieved to discover that the drunken man was ok. He flinched in fear at Brian's outburst, but now he was finding it hard to keep the grin from his blackened face. As Brian fumbled his way back to the track, Saul resisted no longer and grinned in the rain as he rolled away from the tree trunk.

Saul went straight to the den and checked it slowly and deliberately, he knew enough about Russell to realise that he could have re-set the booby trap. He worked his way slowly through the doorway, once inside Saul looked around the den in the stark light of the lamp. He looked into the top of the rucksack nothing seems to have been disturbed. He disconnected the small camera, took it down from the ceiling and stored it in the rucksack. He relaxed into the low chair and took the sandwich box from the bench; he had barely lifted it when he froze the box had been moved, turned around. He distinctly remembered the box facing the other way on the bench, the Star Wars logo on the top was now upside down. Slowly and holding his breath, Saul leaned forward and looked beneath the box he held unmoving just above the bench. The light from the lamp showed nothing unusual beneath. Saul breathed out and leaned back.

All was well, he scolded himself for being so paranoid, no one can make a pressure plate in two minutes and it was only by luck that they had found the den in the first place. Saul took a compact 35-mm fixed focus from the box. The camera was wrapped in tight cling film to protect it from the weather. He checked the lens and batteries for the flash then hung it round his neck. Saul put out the light and listened intently for a few seconds before crawling out from the den. He reached back in and pulled out a helmet, a small bundle of material and finally his side arm from under the canvas chair. Saul hitched the holster strap about his waist and disappeared into the surrounding trees, there were two more photos to get and a princess to save.

He hurried along the track determined to get ahead of Brian.

Russell had moved swiftly around the lake until he came to the path leading up to the house. Heading uphill through the trees he noticed how quiet it was, there was no indication of the storm here. He reached the house looked back and saw that the storm was concentrated over the lake, contained within the natural amphitheatre that made up the landscape. There was little more than light rain and a strong breeze here in the old garden.

23:33

Brian paused on the track wiping the rain from his face, blinking trying to focus on the shadows ahead. He was at the stream, for a second he considered using the stepping-stones; he moved along the bank toward the bridge. He banged the end of the torch the light became a little brighter standing out in the rain. He blinked a few times before stepping on to the plank bridge, the water lapped up to his ankles as he reached the middle. He stopped short of crossing because his torch picked out a figure standing at the end of the bridge barring his way. Through the rain, in the torch light, it took Brian only a few seconds to realise that the figure was A not Russell and B dressed in a black cape and a Darth Vadar helmet.

The cloaked figure stepped forward ignited a light sabre and spoke in a deep voice.

"We have come full circle old man. Return the princess to me."

The cloaked figure wielded the light sabre in a slow menacing arc. Brian pitched sideways in shock, by the time he hit the water he was already scrambling toward the Sith Lord.

"You fucking wanker I'm going to fucking rip your fucking head right off your fucking dark side shoulders."

Saul ran, his heart was thumping at the den, but that was nothing compared to the rush of fight or flight adrenaline. He was so scared; this was no longer a game. He sped along the track frantically trying to switch off the toy light sabre, but the cheap switch had become wet and would not turn out the light.

He ran; excitement and fear giving him massive amounts of energy, any second now he would feel Brian's hand on his shoulder. He whooped and laughed out loud he could not help it, this is so cool he thought. Even over the sound of the intense rain slashing through the trees and his own footfalls, he could clearly hear Brian stamping after him, maybe only a few yards behind. He made his legs go faster. He heard Brian fall and he risked a backwards glance, but he could see nothing, then he was losing it, his lead foot slipped away. He crashed down on one knee and rolled head over heels sliding on the mud. He sprang back up sheer momentum allowed him to carry on running without pause.

He suddenly realised where he was, they were thundering along the track toward the end of the woods. Now, Saul thought, I have the advantage. He knew where he was going and he had a cape, everyone runs faster in a cape.

He tore round the bank jumping roots and ducking the remaining low branches that leapt out to stop him. He heard Brian fall again and risked another look back. No help at all, he could see nothing, he slowed no longer trying to hide the light sabre. Then he was running again with Brian pounding along seconds behind him.

Swearing and stumbling Brian followed, totally fuelled by rage. Twice he had lost traction on the mud, but he was so close. Another branch smacked him in the face spurring him on. Now out on to some open bank and a straight run, he was picking up momentum and getting some wind back. He was gaining on the light.

Just ahead of Saul there was a sharp turn where the track headed back into the trees to avoid the everglades that heralded the start of the reed bed. Saul reached it and threw the light sabre as far as he could into the reeds then dived into the woods.

Brian thumped past him in the dark following the light like a dog after a Frisbee.

00:37

Brian had not noticed the sudden change in undergrowth he stopped and stared about him. How the hell did I get into the reeds, he thought, he was up to his knees in water. The light sabre was stuck in the rushes at head height; he looked all around before pulling it free. He thrashed the sabre about stabbing randomly into the reeds hoping to find Saul hiding close by. He held the sabre above his head trying to pierce the gloom in the pale blue circle of dim light he could see only reeds, he had no idea which way he had come in. The reeds were too tall to allow him any view of the bank, or even a tree. Reeds and black sky were all he could see. He started to make his way in the direction he was sure that the bank lie.

Saul leaned against a thick trunk panting.

"Serves him right," he spat as he watched the blue light move away further into the reeds.

Russell gently closed the tailgate. Collin had wrapped himself in the old blanket and seemed ok. He moved to the house shouting Saul's name, he considered calling his uncle, but decided that at this time of night it would do little to help. He made his way back down the leafy tunnel and around the lake to meet Tom.

As he approached the bivvies something hit him with determined force sending him flying through the air, he landed heavily in the mud the wind knocked from his chest. Someone had tackled him and was now astride him pinning him to the ground.

Tom switched on a powerful torch fixing the beam on Russell's surprised face.

"Bloody hell Russ sorry," he got off immediately. "I thought it was that bloke from the reeds," he helped Russell to his feet. "Where's Brian?"

Russell brushed some wet grass from his clothes and took a few measured breaths.

"He should be here with you by now. I will have to go back and look for him, how are you Tom?"

"I'm fine Russ, sorry about the rugby tackle, I thought I had him for a second there."

Russell told him what had happened on the other side.

"Well he might still be making his way over," Tom said. "He has probably gone the long way round to avoid the reeds or he may have nipped back to the car for something, give him a bit more time. What about Saul, what are you going to do when you find him? If I know Brian he'll break his jaw if he gets hold of him and to be honest I don't blame him. Is Collin ok?"

"Sleeping like a baby in the car, what time is it Tom."

"Sod it, I forgot about my watch," he shook his wrist and tapped the glass face. "It's buggered, but it's well gone midnight. It'll be light in a few hours no chance of finding your cousin till then I wouldn't have thought."

"No, you're probably right Tom let's go round and look for Bri."

Between them they covered the lake and the house again shouting above the wind and rain, Russell showed Tom the den, but Brian was nowhere to be found. Russell and Tom were standing by Collins bivvy, Russell pointed across to the reeds.

"There's only one place left he can be," he said.

"How about the island, could he be on the island?" Tom asked hopefully.

"He didn't like crossing the stream Tom, so there is no way he would have swum out to the island. No, he must be in the reeds."

They spent some time calling out for Brian as they navigated the edge of the huge reed bed.

"Maybe if we get all the torches we could search for him," Tom said.

"Shush . . . did you hear that."

"Wha . . ."

Russell stopped him with his hand. "I'm sure I heard a shout, listen." Russell attempted a few forays into the treacherous reeds shouting for Brian, but each time he came back alone.

"He's in there all right I could just hear him in the middle somewhere. It's hard to tell with the wind whistling over the top of the rushes. I told him to stay where he was, but I don't know if he could hear me."

"Could we set up one of the lights on the end of a rod, hold it up, if he sees it he could work his way toward it."

"Definitely too dangerous, he will be ok if he stays where he is. Moving through those reeds in the dark could easily get you into trouble. No, he must stay put, there's nothing we can do till first light, we may as well get a hot drink."

The light sabre slipped from his hand. Up to his chest in thick weedy water, he watched the blue light fade below the surface of the deep pool in which he was trapped. He made one futile attempt to reach for it, he shouted before pressing on, he could just hear Russell's voice, but had no idea what he was saying.

"TOM, RUSS."

Brian shouted again and tried to move toward Russell. He stopped and listened, Russell seemed further away now, but the wind made it hard to tell. The bottom was starting to give way standing still was not an option. "Clutching at straws clutching at straws." The phrase went relentlessly around Brian's head. His fingertips urgently sought out any kind of support; this was getting very serious, very quickly. Brian was trying to hold down a rising panic, now he could hear Ray Mears whispering in his ear, "Never panic people die when they panic. Never panic people die when they panic." However he was going down, he tried frantically to claw his way through the weed praying for some small purchase at his feet, but the bottom just gave way, he was forced to tread water. Malicious reeds and long evil fronds of slimy weed started to bind themselves around his flagging legs, restricting their movement trapping him, drowning him. His face was barely above the surface, dirty churned up muck was starting to enter his mouth.

It was too late to call for help now. There were tears in Brian's eyes.

Russell made one more trip into the reeds getting as close as he dare to where he thought Brian was then left the reeds for the last time.

"Do you think he heard you Russ?"

"Yes I think he did Tom, I'm convinced that I heard a reply and if he's shouting then he's alive."

"Bloody hell, I didn't even think that he might not be. Is it really that dangerous in there?"

"Yes it is."

13:13

Brian's fingertips rose out of the black water and fell upon solid ground; he burst from the boggy mire gasping and coughing, dragging new air into old smoker's lungs. He started to gag coughing then vomiting thick dirty water. He was on firm ground, but thick reeds blocked his path in all direction other than back into the water. Feeling around him in the dark he orientated himself, it was pitch black he worked out that he was in a narrow five foot clearing along the edge of the bog that nearly claimed his life; he shuffled a little further from the edge. He could only guess that he was deep within the centre of the reed bed where the oldest thickest reeds grew. He shivered despite the heat, the storm whistled overhead, Brian realised that the rain was not reaching him. He shuffled a little more to the right then leaned back on the reeds and wiped mud and tears from his eyes.

It could only be a couple of hours before dawn I will just have to ride it out until then, he thought. Sitting there and waiting until first light was an easy decision to make. At least he was safe and warm, despite the wet clothes and for now at least, out of the storm. Brian felt the firm ground beneath him, patted it in thanks. Exploring his temporary home in the darkness he shuffled his way along the edge, something hard found his hand. Brian tugged at it finally freeing it from the reedy grasp. In the blackness he examined the object. It was some kind of bowl or container, light, but solid, earthenware perhaps. It was obviously broken because Brian could feel a ragged edge on most of the rim, but it was old and worn. He was covered in mud so he crawled to the edge and scooped some of the clearer water from the top with his new bowl. He started to clean himself up, after a few bowls he felt calmer, his heart had finally stopped racing. He fell into an exhausted sleep with the bowl on his lap.

02:30

Tom and Russell sat out of the wind, but in the warm rain it seemed pointless trying to keep dry now. They waited for the water to boil while Tom busied himself with cups.

"This cousin of yours is he a bit mad or what Russ?"

"No not at all, he's a bit like me really."

"Right: that would be a yes then."

The wind whipped around them for a second and dragged away the steam from the kettle. All the rods were out of the water, neither of them felt like fishing.

"Why do you think Brian went into the reeds?"

"I don't know Tom, he must have been following Saul, but that does not make sense because Saul would never cross the reeds at night."

"Why not, he was in the reeds when he got me."

"That was on the edge, once you get to the middle it's very dangerous, only a complete idiot would cross it in the dark and my cousin is not an idiot."

Tom looked up from his mug of tea.

"You've been stuck in there before haven't you?"

"Yes many years ago, it took me hours to find my way out. I was stupid I should have stayed where I was, I nearly drowned."

"I hope he stays put, but why did he go into the bloody reeds in the first place?"

Saul pulled the veil down over his face. Confident that he could not be seen, he peered around the trunk listening to the conversation only a few yards away. He was quite excited and a little nervous. Russell must be really annoyed, he thought. When he heard the shout, he knew at once that he had taken things too far. He could forget about getting a picture. He would be caught if he took it now and that was not an option, not yet, first he must retrieve the princess. For a second he worried about Brian being alone in the reeds, he now knew that Russell had found him, but was unable to get to him. He dismissed the feeling, people can take care of themselves, he thought. The news that Russell had been trapped in the reeds and had managed to walk out in the dark impressed Saul. He knew all too well how difficult that was. He felt a twinge of guilt over Brian he leaned back on the tree and waited. The smell of coffee forced its way through the rain making him feel hungry. There was still an hour until first light he would have to find Brian before Russell if he wanted to save the princess. He slid away from the camp and made his way around the edge of the reeds.

An hour later Russell left Tom asleep in the chair and headed to the reeds determined to find Brian, the rain had stopped and the wind was starting to die down. Tom stirred in the chair his empty cup rolled unnoticed to the floor.

04:06

Bloodshot eyes wide and staring, failing to focus in the mist. The red light provides a powerful beam cutting through the suffocating gloom guiding him as he lurches toward the rod. The reel is frantically back winding faster and faster, line stripping from the spool the butt of the rod starting to sway out of control. The tube of foil is bouncing wildly on the line, the receiver in his pocket screaming for immediate attention.

He knows he will never make it, he knows the old blanket will tangle and twist around his legs, binding them together. He knows that gravity is about to grip him like a bear trap.

He hits the mud at full stretch still hopelessly reaching out to the rod with open hands. The receiver flies spinning from his pocket.

The foil jams against the first eye and thick line springs from the gyrating reel. He tries an impossible, last desperate grab for the rod, his fingertips close around the thin handle, he grips it like a vice. The second of satisfaction is replaced by terror as he is dragged away into the dark cold water, he is unable to release the rod and his cry of triumph turns to screaming bubbles.

Brian woke with a start, thrashing about still screaming.

Thick tall reeds everywhere was all he could see, it was getting light. He stood on unsteady legs trying to improve the view. His heart pounding in his chest made him feel queasy. I could be three feet from the bank and not know it, he thought. Although the rain had stopped, the last of the wind was still rushing above him.

"TOM . . . RUSS," he shouted.

He threw up and wiped his mouth with the hem of his shirt.

"Damn it," he cursed.

A noise to his left in the reeds caught his attention.

"Russ, is that you? I'm over here . . . been here all night."

The noise had stopped. He remembered the bowl; in the half-light, he examined it again. It seemed to be very old, some type of earthenware, very light. He jammed it in his large side pocket then started to force his way through the thick reeds toward the sound. He had travelled less than twenty yards when he fell into a clearing landing on soft dry ground. At first he thought that he had escaped the reeds then realised that he was in a twelve-foot clearing. It was a large nest, no eggs, but heaps of drying reeds built up in the centre and thousands of white feathers. The clearing was circular with only one gap, a narrow path leading down to open water. The reeds here were still very tall Brian walked down the short reed corridor and peered out hoping to see the bank or the island. He was tempted to swim out of the channel, but the water looked very deep at the edge, the reeds stopped quite abruptly. Thoughts of last night came to his mind. He headed back to the nest; there must be another way out he thought. There was something about the noise from the water behind him that made him stop and turn slowly.

A gigantic swan came into view, it rose up hissing, Brian backed down the corridor back into the nest stumbling over the uneven surface. He stumbled, landing with his back against the reeds as the bird entered the clearing. The swan extended its wings and rose to an impressive height. Brian could only think of the swans he used to feed as a child; they didn't seem to like him either. The swan's head swung from side to side looking for other intruders. Seeing none, it advanced.

Two hands grabbed Brian from within the reed wall, he felt himself dragged backwards through the reeds and landed with a thump in a much larger clearing.

Saul scrambled out from under him and immediately checked that Brian was ok. He heard the swan thrashing and hissing behind the reed wall, but it soon gave up. Saul knew that the swan could not get through the reeds so they were safe.

Brian was winded and dazed, he looked up at his saviour. Saul was now wearing light dry combats topped by a brimmed hat. Draped over the hat was a green net that came down over his shoulders. Brian could not make out the face.

"Russ?" he asked.

Saul did not reply, he reached out to Brian's top pocket and took out the figure of the princess.

"Lila," Brian said in a weak voice.

Saul raised a camera to his eye.

"It's Leia. Princess Leia."

As the camera clicked, Brian's attention shifted to something above him, behind Saul. Saul followed his eyes and looked up in time to feel the swan land on his back. The blow knocked him sprawling across the clearing the camera slipped from his grasp it clicked and flashed as it landed. The draft from the wings was sending small debris and feathers flying round the clearing. A wing tip caught Brian in the face: he rolled away to the edge trying to avoid more of the thrashing beak and wings. He huddled against the reeds, the swan practically on top of him. Brian threw up his hands in defence. The reeds behind him came alive for a second time, a large shadow past over him and the swan was gone.

Russell had come through the wall and was grappling with the giant swan. Height meant nothing as swan and man rolled around the clearing, limbs and wings flailing wildly. Saul grabbed Brian's arm, pulling him up and along a path leaving Russell with the swan, but not before recovering the camera and taking two fast snaps of the struggle.

Brian blundered along blindly behind Saul turning left then right completely in Saul's hands. Saul said nothing as he quickly led Brian out of the reeds, as soon as the bank was in sight he ran ahead and disappeared into the trees. Brian shouted after him staggered to the bank and collapsed exhausted on the damp mud.

Russell appeared out of the reeds a few minutes later nursing a cut on his cheek and a huge tear in his shirt.

"Where's Saul?" Russell asked.

"Gone, ran into the trees."

"Are you ok? You look rough."

"Just a bit shaken, did you kill it?"

"No," Russell wiped his cheek and noticed the amount of blood on the back of his hand. "I had better fix this; have you got any cuts Bri?"

"No not really, just a bruise under my eye."

They sat in silence for a few minutes while Russell dressed his wound from a small emergency first aid kit he carried on his belt.

Having spent so much time under bushes and up trees Russell had endured many cuts and grazes over the years, wasp stings, gnats and horseflies. He had twisted or sprained most of his limbs, been slapped in the face by a large common while snorkelling in Oxford, been pushed over by a cow in Devon, chased across fields by numerous horses' cows and goats. He had been perched on by a heron and overrun by rats, been bitten by two dogs and once bitten by an adder.

This may have put off the lesser angler, Russell just learned to be more careful and better prepared. He could now add, wrestled with a giant swan, to his list of animal encounters.

Brian was completely shell-shocked, his hands were shaking he clasped them together. The wind died away the silence was complete. Slowly the sounds of life increased around the lake.

"Rough night," Brian said.

Russell knew that his friend was not exaggerating.

"Come on Bri Let's get dried off and see Tom for a cup of tea."

He led the harrowed Brian back to the bivvies and Tom, who was still asleep in the chair.

06:24

The kettle was whistling Brian emerged from his bivvy in clean dry clothes. Tom poured the water, the sun was coming up and steam was rising from the treetops. Brian set up his chair and slumped into it with a yawn, Tom stirred tea and Russell went to fetch Collin.

Pitcher rolled up behind the Landrover and pulled himself out of the squad car. It was hard to believe the change in the landscape, he remembered the last time that he was here in the garden, thirty odd years ago, the day he swam the lake. He took a long look at the house then headed for the lake, as he passed the back of the hearse he stopped and chuckled. That's amazing, he thought, that bundle still looks like a body. He leaned forward right up to the glass and used his hands to shield the light from around his eyes.

Collin opened one eye and through a small hole in the blanket saw a shadow at the window. He sat up expecting Russell to open the tailgate. Pitcher staggered back falling against the Saab, rolled off the bonnet and on to the grass scrambling for the pepper spray; he heard a voice from the hearse.

"Come on, open up, I feel much better now."

Russell appeared and walked past Pitcher to open the tailgate, Collin climbed out, stretched yawned and pointed.

"Who's that?"

"It's a policeman," Russell said.

"Why is he on the floor?"

They both looked down at the bewildered Pitcher who quickly stood brushing himself down.

"Morning Russell," he said. "I err, sort of tripped on the long grass. I said I might pop in. Have you had a good night?"

Russell retold the events of the night as they walked down the tunnel through the trees. They emerged on to the lake and were greeted by the loud buzz of insects enjoying the calm steamy air. Russell was quite taken with the scene before him it was so different from the night before. It was now hard to imagine the horizontal rain and tornado wind as Russell tried to describe it to Collin and the sergeant. Pitcher made light work of the stepping-stone despite his bulk. They carried on round and stopped at the den; even in the bright morning sun the den was well concealed.

"This could all be seen as assault Russell I have to take it seriously. All of you have grounds for a complaint, I can't say what action will be taken, but he has been in trouble before," Pitcher said.

"Really, what did he do?" Russell sounded surprised.

"Dangerous driving, trespass and failure to stop."

Russell was visibly shocked, he shook his head saying.

"I can't believe it, where did he get the car?"

"Push bike."

"What?"

"He was riding his push bike one of those BMX things. He was doing tricks and stunts around the old quarry in Tynford. One of my constables went over to give him a talking too and throw him out. As you know Russell it's been fenced off for many years, it's very dangerous. Anyway Saul must have seen him coming because as soon as the constable stepped out of his car Saul ran over it to get out."

Collin looked up from the den entrance where he had been peering in.

"What do you mean he ran over it?"

"I mean he ran over it," Pitcher said. "The squad car was blocking the exit Saul hopped on to the bonnet, then the roof and through the gate."

"What carrying his bike?" Russell sounded incredulous.

"No, he was still on his bike," Pitcher continued over Collin's laughter. "There were no real charges laid, but I went over and talked to George, who grounded him for a month."

"Hang on a minute," Collin said. "How old is your cousin Russ?"

"Twelve."

"No! You are kidding."

"No, nearly thirteen or fourteen I can't remember."

Collin roared with laughter.

"I can't see the point in getting him nicked, he's your cousin you sort him out. It sounds like everyone's ok and he's twelve." Collin was looking in the den still chuckling. "He's just having a laugh and to be fair he must be bored stupid living out here in the middle of nowhere. No offence Mr Pitcher."

"Be careful in there Collin," Russell warned as Collin made his way into the den.

"Don't worry about that, after what happened to Brian, I'm not touching anything, hey these photos are really good." Collin backed out of the doorway. Pitcher did not look inside, but took the time to make a few notes in his pocket book. He and Russell strolled around to see Tom and Brian while Collin headed back to his bivvy.

Flashes of memory teased Collin as he approached his Titan, he remembered feeling thirsty and the next minute spitting out water dragging him self on to the bed chair. He had no recollection of Saul. The sleeping bag and bed chair were soaked through; he pulled them out and laid them out in the morning sun. After replacing the rods on the pod, he dug out his spare clothes.

07:39

Collin walked around the lake and arrived to find everyone standing by Tom's bivvy.

"Well he should be bloody punished somehow," Tom said. "That's all I'm saying, I don't care who does it just as long as it bloody happens. How about you Brian, you haven't said anything yet."

"Twelve, he's only fucking twelve, keep the little fucker away from me."

"That's a point Russ, where is he?" Collin asked.

"I know where he is," Russell said.

Pitcher cleared his throat and in a serious tone said.

"Where is he Russell?"

Russell looked up into the tree behind Tom's bivvy.

"Come on Saul, I know you're there."

After a few moments Saul dropped lightly from the tree barely making a sound as he landed, he faced the five men. He removed his hat and veil and stood squinting in the sun. They could all see the family resemblance Saul had the same fine sandy hair and blue eyes, he was tall and thin, his limbs seemingly too long for his torso. He stood silently turning the hat in his hands.

"Saul Black, what have you got to say for yourself?" Pitcher said.

"You little fucker," Brian said and took a step toward the boy.

"Steady Brian," Tom said stepping in front of him. "And mind your language in front of the kid." He couldn't resist any longer he burst out laughing.

"Sod off Tom I nearly drowned because of him." Brian tried to step forward again, but Russell's hand clasped his shoulder and held him firm. Brian shrugged off the hand and kicked at a clump of grass, he pointed at Saul.

"And give me back the princess you little runt," he turned to Russell. "Little Darth Vadar there took your princess Lila. I found her and he stole her."

Everybody looked at Brian, Russell put both hands on Brian's shoulders, he had some experience in calming down distraught relatives. He spoke slowly and deliberately.

"Brian calm down, take a breath. I have no idea what you are talking about. Who is Lila?"

"Princess Lila, from the space film," Brian had a confused look in his eyes.

"Lila," Pitcher said stepping forward. "Do you mean Princess Leia?"

Brian relaxed and stepped back from Russell smiling.

"Of course, yes, Leia," he said. "l. e. i. a. Leia. Princess Leia."

His voice trailed off, he stood staring blankly at the ground completely defeated.

"It's from the star wars film you know. I'm a bit of a fan actually," Pitcher said filling the pause.

Brian slipped away from Russell and charged past Tom, knocking him to the ground. He leaped at Pitcher grabbing his lapels, forcing him back against a tree shaking him in time with his words.

"I KNOW IT'S FUCKING STAR WARS, S. T. A. R. W. A. FUCKING. R. S."

Three of them barely managed to drag the screaming Brian away from the stunned police officer. Pitcher recovered himself and within seconds had Brian in handcuffs. As soon as the old-fashioned cuffs clicked shut Brian calmed down and stood dejected in front of the policeman.

"I'm sorry Russell," Pitcher said. "But I am going to take him in for his own good he's obviously in some sort of shock. I will get back to you later and let you know what's happening. I will have the doc take a look at him on the way in." He started to lead Brian away. "As for Saul I will leave it up to you."

Brian offered no resistance as Pitcher led him away. The others patted him on the back and added words of encouragement shaking their heads.

"He's bloody disappeared again," Tom said looking all around. "Russ, where's Saul?"

"Gone, he ran off when Brian lost it."

"You saw him go. You let him go. Why did you let him go?"

"Forget it Tom, let's sit down and have some breakfast."

"Come on we could still catch him he can't have got far."

"Tom it's over; let him go, he's not going to do anything. It's over, forget it." There was an edge in Russell's voice.

125

"Fine . . . fine. I'll put the kettle on then."

"I've just had a thought," Collin said. "Does, going mad assaulting a policeman and getting arrested disqualify Brian from the competition?"

Tom and Russell looked at each other and shook there heads.

"No," they said in unison.

"Because he has had the biggest fish so far," continued Collin. "And no offence to Brian, but I do not intend to loose my twenty five quid. It's not our fault that he got himself arrested, we've all had a rough night. I say we carry on."

"We may as well Russ," Tom said. "Brian will be fine and you know what he will bloody say if we cancel the bet when he was winning. He will bang on about it forever we will have to pay him just to shut him up."

"Of course, why not, but let's have some breakfast first I'm starving," Russell said breaking into a grin.

The plan was to evacuate and take the wrap later. It had been easy to slip away when Brian had attacked Pitcher. He stayed hidden crouching in the bushes listening. He was relieved that the police would not be calling on his dad, but he was sure that Russell would be telling his father. This could mean grounding for the rest of the holidays. On the other hand there were three rolls of film to be developed and the last few snaps should prove very interesting. As soon as he heard Russell say that they were going to have breakfast Saul decided to make his move. He slipped away from the group and headed for the den. He took the long way around deliberately taking his time staying off the path afraid that he may be spotted. He watched and waited to make sure that Pitcher and Brian had left the lake.

Saul scrambled down the steep bank to reach the den; he crawled in and sat down. Switching on the lamp did little to improve the gloom. One by one he took down the photos and stored them in a large envelope; he put them in the rucksack. He collected all of his things and stuffed them in the rucksack, spare clothes, his cape and mask, the star wars sandwich box, boots, a thermos flask, burner and kettle.

He crawled out dragging the sack. Slinging the weighty bulk on to his back he shrugged it into place and clipped up the support belt. He took one step and froze.

Balanced on the fallen trunk before him, the very log that he had clung to in the storm last night, was his light sabre. He crouched down his eyes darted around the clearing from tree to bush looking for Russell's outline. The wood was thick in front of the den and the early light did not yet have the height to penetrate the trees with any real success.

Saul turned it over in his mind, the sabre wasn't there when he arrived, or was it? Russell could have done it when he left the reeds earlier. He was preoccupied when he had returned to the den perhaps he did not see it. No, it was definitely not there when he came back.

Saul was thrilled; at last he could pit his wits against Russell. Carefully he inched his way toward the fallen tree on his hands and knees feeling for trip wires or pressure switches among the leaves. He stopped short of the light sabre pausing to study the area surrounding it. Using a handy branch he disturbed the air above and around the toy seeking out wires or sensors, there were no signs of a booby trap. The only thing that continued to worry Saul was the piece of paper wrapped around the sabre handle, secured with a rubber band. It could only be from Russell and therefore must be treated with extreme caution.

He stayed in the crouched position the pack was weighing him down, he felt like a long legged turtle. Using the branch Saul knocked the light sabre from the log and crouched a little lower, no lights no cameras nothing. He spun round hoping to catch someone watching or sneaking up behind him, the weight of the pack nearly took him off his feet. There was nothing there other than the thick bushes, trees and the empty den. Very cautiously he picked up the light sabre and pulled the note from the handle. The large spider writing did not make sense, it just said 'don't look up.'

Saul looked up.

Click

He threw himself to the side, but it was too late and he knew it. The second his head tilted up his brain screamed, *DON'T LOOK RUN YOU IDIOT*, but he could not help himself the power of curiosity was about to kill the cat. By the time the message to move had arrived at his feet the trap had been sprung. He lay unmoving where he had landed face down under the weight of the rucksack. He was cursing himself, beaten by such simple reverse psychology. How did the camera go off at the right time? There were no wires or sensor; he heard a sound away to his left.

"How did you do it," he called out. He knew that it could only be Russell.

Russell dropped lightly from a nearby tree and stood looking down at Saul.

"Remote control for the camera," he said. "Essential kit when fishing solo and very handy it seems, for beating cousins at their own game." He reached up and took down the camera concealed high up in an overhanging branch.

"Oh by the way a couple of my friends would like to have a word with you."

Tom and Collin emerged from where they had been hiding on the edge of the small clearing. Each man had branches and twigs secured to his clothing, their faces were streaked with brown and green. Huge smiles stood out from behind fronds and small branches fastened to their hats. They joined Russell and stood looking down at the boy. Saul rolled over and tried to sit up, but the weight of the rucksack pinned him to the floor like a beetle on its back, there was no chance of getting away. All three captors raised their cameras.

"Wait, wait, there's big fish, big big fish, a big common," Saul blurted out.

The cameras stayed raised.

"I can tell you where to find it."

"Hold up let him speak, there might be something to salvage after all," Collin said lowering his camera. "What big common?"

"There's two of em, they swim round the island and they are huge." Saul relaxed a little as the other cameras were lowered. "The biggest one I've seen must weigh thirty pounds. I've been trying out baits all summer. I found one they like."

"What is it, what have you been feeding them on?" Collin said.

"I'll only tell you if you promise to let me go," Saul looked straight at Russell. He used the look he gave his dad when he was trying to avoid grounding.

Tom and Collin sensed that this was Russell's decision. Russell peered down at the young face, a practised picture of remorse and repentance.

"You gave Brian a very rough night," Russell said. "You owe him a big apology . . . Ok, what bait is it Saul?"

A tide of relief washed away the tension round Saul's eyes leaving only a hint of a smile on the lips.

"Peanuts, I've been feeding them peanuts."

"I've got peanuts," Collin said, he was instantly excited. He slapped Tom on the back. "Tom I've got peanuts with me."

Saul had struggled to his feet.

"Can I go now?"

Russell studied his face for a few seconds more then nodded. Russell and Tom moved toward the trees, but Collin stayed and barred Saul's exit, Saul looked down. Collin grabbed Saul's shirt and leaned in close, almost nose to nose.

"You were lucky last night little man, if Brian had got hold of you he would have punched first and checked your birth certificate after."

Saul tensed himself ready to run. Collin patted Saul's shoulder and smiled.

"So where exactly on the island have you been feeding these peanuts?"

"Come on Collin, let's go back and have breakfast," Tom called out.

A minute later Collin let Saul go and watched him scamper off into the woods as fast as his rucksack would let him. Collin caught up with the others.

"He said that they swim round the island for most of the day and he's fed nuts on all four sides, but most of the takes come from under the lightning tree." The other two looked at him. "Well that's what he called it. I wondered if I could move over with you Tom."

"Sure you can plot up in Brian's swim."

08:58

Tom pushed the bread around the plate soaking up the last of the tomato juice and bacon fat.

"Mmm Bloody hell that was worth the wait," he said.

He popped the nub of bread into his mouth then dropped the bare plate to the ground and picked up his mug of coffee.

"I hope Brian's ok, what do you think Russ; what do you think will happen?"

"He's in good hands Tom, Pitcher is a good man and he said that he would let me know, but I doubt that anything official will happen."

"But Russ, he attacked a policeman, he knocked his bloody hat off. If you did that back home the old bill would kick your arse all the way to the station. And then have the front to nick you for assault when you got there."

"Pitcher said that he would see the doctor then let him sleep it off. There is also one thing that I know about Pitcher that goes in Brian's favour. He hates paperwork, really hates it and last night means a ton of it."

Pitcher peered over the rim of his mug slowly dragging his eyes over the rows of old files that ran the length of the long shelves lining the walls of his tiny office. The blind was down allowing striped light to fall on the dusty tomes, making the bow in the overloaded shelves all the more obvious. One of the new constables had pointed out that all this could be transferred to a few computer discs. Even though Pitcher's loathing for paperwork was legendary, it was overshadowed by his ignorance and mistrust of computers. He had resisted the modern urge to reduce data to a series of ones and zeros, preferring to thumb paper and card. He understood paper and index cards he did not understand megabytes and gigabits. It was his years as a police officer, his years of experience that weighed down those shelves. A shadow drew his eyes to the glass panel in the door. There was a sharp rap on the frame, the door handle turned.

"What is it Baker?" Pitcher snapped.

Baker stood uneasily in the doorway.

"Sorry to disturb you Sergeant, but that bloke you put in number six where did you say you found him?"

"I told you Baker he had a rough night fishing on old Mac's lake. Give him breakfast and a blanket and let him get some rest."

"We found something in his property we think you should see sir."

"Baker, if you are about to tell me that he has some cannabis or funny little pills forget it. I'm taking him back to the lake after lunch. Why do we have his possessions? He's not under arrest."

"Insurance sir."

"What?"

"He is in the book under suspicion of vagrancy sir."

"Why?"

"Insurance sir, otherwise we have to fill out one of the blue forms. If we arrest him we only have to fill out two pink ones."

"That's ridiculous: well done."

"Yes sir, thank you sir, but that's not the point, the point is in his possessions. The nurse came by to check him over; he's fine by the way, just suffering from shock and a bit of exposure. Recommends he goes home to bed, reminds me of my brother when he came back from that survival course he did when he was in th . . ."

Pitcher was winding his hand in a circular motion indicating his desire for Baker to get to the aforementioned point.

"Sorry sir, anyway I was talking to the nurse in the evidence room when she noticed the possessions on the table. We thought it was a bit of old pot, but she recognised it straight away. She's a bit of an archaeologist on the side, in fact she knows my sister's ex husband. He's involved with the local archi . . ."

Pitcher held up a hand.

"Baker, what the hell are you talking about?"

"The skull sir. He had a human skull in his pocket . . . well a bit of one anyway."

Pitcher closed his eyes and let out a long sigh. Behind the closed lids he could visualise the paperwork teetering on his desk then slowly falling, increasing in mass, drowning him in a torrent of pink grey and blue. He watched himself washed out through the doorway and down the corridor waving to his colleagues as the tide swept him away to a heaving sea where he would drown in swirling reams of endless depth.

09:26

" **I** can see them heading clockwise, slowly going round the tip of the island," Russell said. He climbed down dropping the last six feet landing lightly next to Collin. "It will not be easy from this distance. I don't think that you'll get a decent presentation. The bottom seems to slope away gradually from the island then it steps down quite sharply into what looks like about four feet of water. The carp seem to hug the shelf occasionally picking bits out of the shallow water. Did you have any success out there yesterday Tom?"

"We both had a rod on it, Brian managed to get a foot or so from the island, I stopped mine about ten feet short. I had . . ."

"Let me guess," Russell cut in. "You had nothing big, maybe the odd small carp, Brian had lots of liners and the occasional empty run, but caught nothing."

"Bang on, I had two runs both were small mirrors and Bri had nothing, but his buzzer didn't stop all afternoon. We tried a few different rigs, pva bags, stringers; we couldn't work out what was happening. We had plenty of fish away from the island on the other rods. But we could see big fish moving out there so we stuck it out."

"It was your position Tom," Russell said. "You were too far away to tempt the bigger fish from the shelf and Brian's mainline would have been in mid water as his lead was sitting up on the top of the shelf. It would have been in plain sight. Big fish would have gone round it and smaller fish would have brushed past it giving the liners and false runs."

"Makes sense to me," Collin joined in. "I watched all of the Korda DVDs. I would have fished a slack line with a braid hook length pinned down every couple of inches with a bit of heavy metal. Maybe a lead core leader, two-ounce flat lead to stop the roll on the slope, used a back lead to pin down the line. I agree with Russ presentation is key to a lake like this."

"You're right Collin, but that isn't quite what I meant," Russell said. "Besides that, there are fundamental flaws in your set up and you're ignoring the obvious."

"What do you mean fundamental flaws" he replied indignantly. "What's wrong with the rig?"

"The island is about sixty yards out," continued Russell. "The flat lead is a good idea, but they are notorious for tangles at a distance. The chances of everything on the rig landing perfectly are slim. You will have little or no control of the presentation regardless of your attempts to pin it all down. Even if it all lands ok, the slack line will let you down. You would have no bite indication, as you say you've seen the DVDs, you know how easily bait can be ejected. The slack line rig only works effectively at very short distances."

Russell's comprehensive trashing of his rig plan ruffled Collin.

"Ok so I tweak the rig a bit," he said. "But we can't do anything about the distance can we."

"As I said, you are ignoring the obvious," Russell said pointing to the island.

Collin stared blankly across the water.

"You're kidding, as soon as they see us swim out they will bugger off."

Russ thought for a moment, Collin was right, if they spooked the fish it could be hours before they returned to the island if at all.

"Ok, maybe not from here," he said. "The nearest point to the island is on the far side at the head of the stream, it's only thirty yards. That's half the distance. It would only take a few minutes to swim; I reckon we could make the island while the carp are on this side as they circle it. They will not see us if we are quick. As I remember it's five or six feet deep for most of the way across, but there are a few deep holes."

"Hang on, how the hell am I going to get my tackle out there," Collin said, looking horrified. "I can't swim with this lot on my back."

"You won't need it," Tom said. "We will only need a few bits just grab some essentials and a handful of bait, throw them in a plastic bag."

"Plastic bag! You have got to be kidding, I've got two thousand quids worth of tackle here and you want me to chuck it in a bin liner."

"Well at least come and have a look first, see if it's possible to get a rod out," Tom said.

09:33

Brian stretched out on the basic vinyl covered mattress and yawned, he sat up pushing the rough blanket aside. The loose shirt and baggy trousers that the police had given him, to replace his damp combats, were making his arms and legs itch. Diffused sunlight was forcing its way through the tiny cell window and discovering that it was not really worth all the effort. The door was ajar, there were distant voices floating up the corridor beyond, the door swung open. Pitcher strolled in and immediately sat down on the chair he was carrying.

"Hello Brian how are you feeling?" he said.

"I'm so sorry," Brian blurted out.

"Stop," Pitcher said. "You are not being charged with anything, you are not in trouble and you are free to go as soon as you have answered a couple of quick questions."

Brian was visibly relieved.

"Thank you I appreciate that," he said.

"Can you remember much about last night?"

"Some of it, but most of the details are a bit hazy."

"You were quite lucky by all accounts. I have decided to take no official action against young Saul Black, but if you decide that you want to pursue it I will back you all the way," he paused hoping that the answer would be no.

"No, no I am sure Russ will sort it out."

"Ok then I am going back to the lake in about an hour in the meantime I will have some breakfast sent in and you are free to wander around, but do not get under Bakers feet or you're likely to get trampled in a stampede of useless information." He stood to leave then paused with his hand on the back of the chair.

Brian sensed that Pitcher was hovering.

"Is there anything else you need to know?" he said.

"Yes as a matter of fact there is, do you remember what you had in your pockets earlier today?"

"No, well um a couple of leads, maybe a bit of rig tubing."

"Nothing else?"

"Oh there was a little pot thing like a big egg, I think I may have put that in my pocket, but to be honest it's a bit of a blur."

"Where did you get it?"

"What, the egg? I found it when I was in the reeds."

"Would you remember where in the reeds?"

"Why?"

"Would you?"

"I doubt it, like I said it's all a bit of a blur. Russell might know or maybe that kid, why?"

"Ok thank you Brian, I am going back to the lake in an hour I will take you back then." Pitcher left the door ajar, Baker was in the corridor.

"Did you tell him sarge, what did he say, did he say where he got it?"

"Slow down Baker. Take the bone over to the hospital for testing and tell them I want it done straight away. As soon as they know what it is tell them to phone me direct. I'm not going to send in the troops for a dogs head or a cow or something. Until then we wait."

"Bloody hell," Tom said as he spat out some more weedy water. "This is harder than I thought it would be."

Russell was gliding easily through the water he stopped and looked back treading the water gently bobbing making hardly a ripple.

"Did you take off your boots Tom? It's a lot easier with bare feet."

"I did, but they're still dragging me down."

"Why?"

"They're round my neck."

Tom's head ducked under once again. Collin was close behind him.

"My god Tom you're a doughnut sometimes, he meant leave your boots on the bank," Collin said.

Russell reached out, took the boots from around Tom's neck and draped them over his own shoulder. Then he struck out for the island. Five feet from it he stood on the bottom, the water came to his shoulders. He waited for Tom and helped him toward the island. It was another two feet before Tom's feet found the weedy bottom. He scrambled on to the island immediately turning to assist Russell. Collin swam right to the edge and easily pulled himself out.

Only Russell noticed the flattened grass where Saul had been laying the day before. He scouted the water margin and waited only a minute before a group of large carp come round the bank. The carp stopped for a few seconds at the muddy section of water where they had crossed, then continued un-fussed. Their landing had been an undiscovered success. They moved toward the centre of the island.

10:38

Pitcher raised the phone to his ear.

"Yes ... are you sure? Bugger, keep it there I will send someone over," he replaced the receiver. "Baker," he shouted.

Promptly the shadow appeared at the door.

"Yes sir?"

"Go back to the hospital and bag it as evidence then meet me at Mac's old place."

"Corr I can't believe it sir, a real skull, did they say how old it is? How did it end up in the lake, was it murder sir? Corr it's just like silent witness sir."

Pitcher was momentarily lost again in his vision of paperwork.

"Baker; on your way out will you open a new box of pens and tell Janice at the library that we are going to need her photocopier."

11:02

"**K**eep still Collin" Tom said in a low whisper.

They were laying side-by-side trying to peer through a slim gap in the dense grass at the waters edge.

"Sorry Tom I'm trying to see over to the left a bit. Can you see the bottom?"

"Yes clearly and I can tell you now that they don't like Brian's boilies. I can see his boilies in little lines just as they must have landed on the stringers. They are completely untouched. I can't see any peanuts though, but you can tell that fish have been feeding here, look at the bare patches."

Collin slid himself back from the edge, sat up and pulled clear a plastic bag full of peanuts from his pocket.

"Hey where's Russ?"

Tom looked behind him then up.

"He's in the tree," he whispered.

"How the hell did he get up there without us seeing? Russ, what can you see," he called out in the hoarse whisper.

Russell was lying along the denuded tree trunk motionless and silent. Slowly Russell raised his hand and held up three fingers, then a clockwise circular motion. Collin took this to mean three carp coming from the left. Russell held up four then five fingers.

"Should be five carp coming from the left Tom, can you see them?" whispered Collin.

"Can't see them yet, wait yes, I can see them. Wow, you have to see this."

Collin crawled back to the slim gap and Tom shuffled over to allow him a better view.

"Jesus Christ," whispered Collin. "That one in the middle must be thirty plus, it's massive."

The two leading carp, both mid twenties, arrived at the strings of bait left by Brian's rigs. They started to nose the boilies disturbing the lines and mouthing the baits moving a short distance then ejecting them. They went along the lines until all were broken up. A twenty plus common moved along the margin then seemingly at random it picked up one of the boilies and savoured it for almost a minute before ejecting it into the deeper water. This appeared to be some kind of signal because within a few minutes the five carp had picked up and ejected all of the boilies into the deeper water. The carp drifted along the margin then as one turned into open water and swiftly disappeared from view.

Collin was the first to speak.

"If I hadn't seen that with my own eyes I wouldn't have believed it."

Russell was still in the tree, from there, he could make out the house and some sort of activity in the garden; he recognised the unmistakable blue flash of emergency lights.

"Something's going on up at the house," he called down. "I think we should go back and find out, this looks important."

Waiting only for Collin to throw in a few handfuls of soaked peanuts they returned to the mainland and headed back to the house.

Four police officers met them when they reached the tunnel leading to the house. Two were wearing white coveralls and were carrying hard-cases of equipment. Two uniformed officers were pulling a trailer on which were a flat bottom punt and more equipment including some scuba tanks. At the rear of the crew walked Pitcher carrying his lunch and looking a bit odd in a pair of ancient canvas waders. By his side walked Brian.

The crew busied themselves setting up tables and a generator, the equipment was unloaded and the punt launched on to the lake. Leaving the two men in uniform to finish on the bank the two others boarded the punt and waited.

They were all glad to see that Brian was ok. Pitcher explained that he wanted Russell to lead him into the reeds to the spot where Brian had been last night. The idea was to guide the boats in as close as possible then allow the officers to search the area as best they could. As Russell was going to be busy Tom Collin and Brian retreated to the bivvies, Brian had no desire to return to the reeds and after all Pitcher had said that it was fine to carry on fishing as long as they stayed away from the search area. They decided to go stalking around the other side of the lake where Collin still had a stack of beer; the day was turning out to be a scorcher.

12:12

After giving the officers in the boat a few instructions Russell led Pitcher into the reeds, as they made their way, Russell took the time to point out some of the more treacherous areas. They zig zagged their way through the reeds, by the time they arrived at the swan's nest they could hear shouting ahead. Russell stepped into the clearing and was greeted by an explosion of white wind as the swan flew up past him crashing a second later into some lesser reeds to his right.

One of the boat crew was kneeling down in the clearing there was a large rip in his white coverall and he was looking a bit dazed while nursing a bleeding wound on his hand. The dust settled and Pitcher entered the nest, he looked over at the swan that had chosen to remain close by. The swan glared back.

"How long do swans live?" Pitcher asked.

Russell was helping the officer dress his wounded hand using the first aid kit from his belt.

"I don't know, fair time I imagine?" he replied.

"Doesn't matter. Right where do we go from here Mr Black?"

13:03

" **T**his is where I found Brian," Russell said. "And from what he told me, he only travelled a short distance from where he spent the night."

Pitcher stared at the reed walls surrounding them turning a full 360 degrees. The only way into the clearing seemed to be by boat or the way that they had forced their way through. He turned to the officer with the injured hand.

"Go and get that looked at, find Brian Redcar and tell Trevor to bring him out here."

The officer walked off toward the boat.

"He won't remember anything," Russell said.

"He will have to," Pitcher said with a professional edge to his voice.

"He won't, but Saul will he was here before me; he pulled Brian out of the nest. He would never have come here without good reason, because of the swan. So he must have known where Brian was."

Pitcher was already walking down the reed corridor toward the departing boat. He shouted out across the water.

"Forget Brian Redcar, find Saul Black." He returned to the nest to find Russell crouching, peering at bits of broken reed around the edge of the nest. "Found anything?"

Russell looked up shaking his head.

"It's hard to say there's so much damage from the fight that I can't . . ."

"What fight?" Pitcher cut him short.

"With the swan."

"Who had a fight with a swan?"

"Me and I wouldn't recommend it."

Pitcher was shaking with silent laughter. He could see the swan now drifting in open water by the entrance to its nest; he brought his mind back to the task in hand.

"We will just have to take pot luck till we can get Saul out here," Pitcher grumbled.

"Give me a few minutes it's all starting to make a bit more sense," Russell said.

Pitcher looked up, the sun was rising higher it was fast becoming very hot. He took a seat on the edge of the nest where it was quite dry, he unhitched his waders and slid them down and unbuttoned his shirt; it was going to be a long day, he thought.

As Russell poked about the clearing Pitcher closed his eyes thinking again about retirement. Russell's voice dragged him back.

"I'm just going to step through here I will be back in a minute or two," Russell said. "I may have found the path he took."

"Shout if you need me Russell," Pitcher called back over his shoulder, he closed his eyes again.

"Can you see anything?" Collin asked standing just behind Tom.

"No I saw one of the guys in the white suits go in and then come out and now he's going back to the bank. That copper shouted something, but I didn't get what it was, I think he said something about Saul."

"Come on then, Brian's finished sorting out his tackle," Collin said. "We thought about trying the stream."

They marched off to where Brian was waiting with his net over his shoulder.

The sun was now peeking over the tallest of the reeds Pitcher was enjoying the warmth on his face, he could hear Russell in the reeds behind him, but then a noise in front. Without moving his body, he raised one eyelid a fraction. He watched and waited for a few more seconds then sprang forward thrusting his hands through the reeds grasping the shadow he had seen. Satisfaction on his face as he got a handful of cotton fabric, he pulled with all his bulk. Saul popped from the reeds like a cork and landed sprawling at Pitcher's feet.

"Nice of you to join us young Mr Black," Pitcher said using his smug policeman's voice.

Behind them, Russell pulled himself from the reeds surprised at what he saw.

"I have found it," he proclaimed. "I know where Brian spent the night." He walked across to Pitcher and stood looking down at Saul. "We could have done with you ten minutes ago. Have you been home yet?"

"I have, but I came back when I saw the Police coming down the lane. Why do you want to know where he spent the night?"

Pitcher reached down and pulled Saul upright.

"Come on both of you, show me where."

Russell, Saul and Pitcher squeezed themselves into the reeds. It took twenty minutes to cover twenty yards having to force their way between hardened reed stems. Pitcher thrust his head through the last of the reeds. He could see the small clearing on the edge of a wide pool of weedy water surrounded by tall reeds. There was nothing obvious at a glance, but then Pitcher wondered what it was that he had expected to see. He could make out some gouges in the bank and could clearly see Brian's footprints. With a start he realised that the deep gouging must have been caused by Brian frantically dragging himself out.

He noticed something poking out of the reeds down by his foot; in fact, he was standing on it, he crouched down to inspect it. He had to force the reeds apart to get a clearer view. It was the end of a small bone; he lifted his foot to reveal some other smaller bones barely visible amongst the reed roots. One of the bones caught his eye with a glint of something metallic. He reached down and picked it up; it was a ring. As he lifted it, a small bone slid from within. It was a wedding band; Pitcher took the ring and placed it in his shirt pocket.

"Damm it," he said under his breath. "Thank you lads for all your help, Russ do you think it's possible to get a boat out to here."

"No."

They made their way back to the swans nest, the boat had returned and a white suited officer was waiting for them. Pitcher was amused to notice that the officer had a baseball bat with him. Using tape from the boat Pitcher and Russell marked out the rout to the body.

"Right," Pitcher said. "Thanks again for all your help. We will take it from here. We'll remove the body today there's no real need to close the lake so you are free to carry on fishing. Just stay away from us, needless to say." He looked directly at Saul, who turned away embarrassed.

"How are you going to remove the deceased?" Russell asked with professional curiosity.

Pitcher rubbed his chin.

"Good point Russell, but I do have a plan."

With that, he left with the officer. Russell and Saul made their way back to the bank to the other three fishermen.

13:36

Pitcher was leaning back in the small boat talking on his radio as a white suited officer managed the oars.

"Yes, patch me through . . . thank you . . . Hello Mr Black, Sergeant Pitcher here . . . Very well thank you, I am down at Mac's old place; in fact I am on the lake as we speak. I am coming up to see you now . . . no . . . no he is not in trouble, actually he has been quite useful in a round about way. I will see you in twenty minutes . . . ok."

The boat bumped and scraped against the muddy bottom as the craft reached the bank. Pitcher stood and steadied himself before moving along the boat toward the bow just behind white suited officer.

As the first man put a foot on the bank, the swan appeared diving out of the sun, swooping down in an arc so low that both men had to duck. Pitcher reached for the baseball bat, but the first officer lost his balance and fell forward into the water kicking the boat backwards as he did so. Pitcher fell and landed heavily in the boat, banging his head on the bench seat. He sat up rubbing his brow and swearing. The first officer was already wading back to take control of the boat. Pitcher allowed him to tow in the boat while he watched the swan drift back toward the entrance to its nest. The swan glowered back.

14:05

"Why did you lie?" Russell said, as he and Saul walked round to the stream.

"I didn't; about what?"

"The bait."

"What bait?"

Russell stopped to look at his cousin.

"Don't play games with me Saul, you should know better."

"Sorry Russ, I thought I will have to tell them something so I chose peanuts, because I have never tried them and well I . . ."

Russell held up a hand.

"I was just a little bit hurt that you lied to me."

"I didn't really, I told the truth about where the big common goes she does spend time round the island with a few other very big commons so I only lied about the bait and their favourite feeding spot and I said most of that to the tackle man when he cornered me earlier." Saul took a long breath after the sentence. Russell had to laugh.

They carried on around the lake after a little while Saul spoke.

"Why didn't you ask me what the real bait is?"

"I don't need to."

Russell stopped to watch two carp in the small bay ahead of them. Saul pointed across to the open water where a very large carp had broken the surface.

"How can you know?" he said as they carried on.

Russell did not answer. They approached the head of the stream in time to see both Brian and Collin with fish on the bank while Tom fussed around them with the scales. Russell turned to Saul to find him gone, a second or two later he spotted him crouching amongst the trackside undergrowth; he crouched down next to him.

"Don't worry Saul, he will be fine, but you must apologise, it's time for you to grow up a little bit."

They walked toward the three anglers, Collin was laughing.

"This is too easy, that's the second one in half an hour. Hi Russ."

Tom looked up and then at Brian, then Saul, then Brian.

Brian stood and took a step toward Saul, Russell nudged Saul forward. Saul reluctantly took a step then stopped with his head down. Brian took another step forward, Saul shuffled forward another few inches.

"Oh for god's sake it's like bloody line dancing," Tom said exasperated.

"I am sorry," Saul said. "And I'm glad you didn't drown and stuff."

Brian just nodded, then he realised that he still had the fish in his hands.

"I had better put this back," he said.

That seemed to be the end of it so Collin took the opportunity to quiz Saul about the island. They all walked back to Tom and Brian's bivvies. Collin was walking ahead with Saul, deep in conversation. Every now and again Saul would look back over his shoulder with a pained look on his face.

14:32

Pitcher was driving back to the lake now that he had managed to borrow the equipment he needed. He glanced round to the back seat hoping that it did not leak on the upholstery, as he pulled into the garden he was straight on the radio. He parked up and waited. Five minutes later three officers came up the path from the lake pulling the boat trolley. Pitcher instructed the men to collect a dozen long planks, which were resting against the house and take them down to the water. He dragged the equipment from the back of the car, annoyed to find a small oil spot left on the seat. Giving the equipment to one of the men, he strolled ahead while trying on the thick gloves.

At the lake he had the planks tied together and floated out on the lake. Pitcher got in the boat with the equipment, a white suited officer started to row them toward the swan nest while towing the planks behind the punt.

Pitcher remained in the boat while the other officer went ahead with the baseball bat. A few seconds later he came running back.

"All clear sir," he said, then helped Pitcher with the machine. They dragged the planks ashore and the officer went back for another man. Pitcher stayed in the sun perched on the nest until two officers came up the reed corridor carrying some of the planks.

Pitcher pulled on the close fitting headgear and pulled on the chunky toggle, the engine roared into life.

15:16

Tom had decided on an early lunch of sandwiches and soup. Tom had put Saul to work making the 'sarnies' as he called them, while he tended to the soup. The other three were huddled in Brian's bivvy looking at fish photos on their cameras and Brian was totting up the score so far.

"One fish: is that all?" Collin said. "I thought you were good at this." He was ribbing Russell. "Even Brian has more than that and he's spent most of his time getting lost or being arrested."

"Actually Cole', I have the most weight and the biggest fish so far," Brian cut in. "I beat Russ by one pound with a twenty five pound mirror."

Collin snatched the paper from Brian's hand.

"Are you sure Bri, hang on! I'm below Tom, how come?"

Brian took the paper back.

"We all agreed that nothing under fifteen pounds will count. Actually it was your idea, remember that night in your tackle room. Just before we left you came up with the idea so that we wouldn't be tempted to go tiddler bashing as you called it," he laughed.

"Did I? I don't remember that. Hang on yes, I did say that, sod it."

"What the bloody hells that," Tom said, when he heard the roar of the engine.

They all piled out of the bivvy.

"That's a chain saw," Russell said.

"That's my dad's chain saw," Saul said.

Pitcher was pleased with himself for having started the chain saw on the first pull; he revved the trigger and allowed the engine to settle to a steady throb. He pulled down the plastic face protector with a thick gloved hand, a curt nod to the other officers indicated that he was about to start. He knelt down and thrust the saw into the reeds just above the roots. As the reeds tumbled the other officers pulled them clear. After a couple of yards of clearing a path three feet wide Pitcher retreated allowing the planks to be laid down. They repeated the process and each time the saw complained a little more. The reeds were getting thicker and older as he worked his way toward the body.

When he was sure that they were only a few feet away, he stopped and walked back to the nest for a rest. They had been cutting for nearly an hour and Pitcher was sweating heavily. The safety visor continually steamed up when he bent down reducing visibility to practically nothing. Not ideal when wielding a chain saw. The officers appeared carrying bundles of reed, taking their cue from Pitcher they sat down and silently brushed reed dust from their white coveralls.

"I knew the lady that we are about to find," Pitcher said quietly. "Not very well, but met her, knew her face. We came here in nineteen sixty-eight looking for this woman and we failed to find her. I failed her. Today we can do something to help put that right and we should do that with all the respect that she deserves."

They walked silently down the makeshift path and stood at the last few feet of reed wall. He pulled down the visor and started the chain saw.

Pitcher knelt down and started cutting, the reeds were at their thickest here determinedly resisting the chain. The facemask was already misting up as he thrust the blade back in dodging his head out of the way as the officers pulled back the reeds. One more thrust and Pitcher realised that he must be through, the last of the reeds fell away to reveal a very large raging white swan.

Pitcher could not see the swan because of the dust and the misted facemask, but he knew something was up because the two officers instantly dropped their reeds and retreated up the path they had made.

Pitcher stood up, the swan attacked. It flew up in front of him, narrowly avoiding the saw, thumping into Pitcher's chest sending him backwards down onto the planks. The swan was on his chest fiercely pecking at the facemask. Pitcher was completely unprepared for this kind of assault, he tried to fend the animal off with his left arm, but the drumming on the facemask was relentless, each impact sent pitcher's head slamming into the planks beneath him. He tried to lift the chain saw still in his right hand, but the hand guard had snagged in the fallen reeds, he struggled with the saw.

All the while the swan was making progress on the plastic facemask a large crack appeared across the length of the Perspex. Pitcher's eyes were starting to close he was blacking out, the facemask was torn away.

There was a shout and a whooshing sound as the baseball bat hit the swan. A shadow came over him as a white suited officer stood above. Pitcher sat up, shook his head and stood looking around for the swan.

It lay on the planks in front of him looking up with one eye; blood was running from one side of its beak. Pitcher retrieved the chain saw from the reeds, the engine was still chugging away steadily, he turned to the officers behind him.

"What took you so long," he shouted. "That thing nearly had my eye out."

One of the officers pointed behind Pitcher. He swung his bulk round at speed, in the corner of his eye he saw the swan leaving the ground for another assault, only this time there was no facemask. Pitcher threw up his arms to defend himself, as he pulled the weighty saw round the thick gloves caught on the trigger.

The machine roared as it collided with the swan, Pitcher lost his grip on the handle, there was no choice, he dived to the side.

Swan and saw fell to the ground in a loud explosion of blood and feathers. The chain saw jammed and screeched to a halt buried in the swan carcass; there was silence. Pitcher crawled back on to the planks helped by one of the white suited officers their suits now sporting splashes of blood and bits of swan. He looked down at his own shirt and was surprised to find part of a foot stuck to it. He flicked it off and stood looking down at the swan. He grabbed the chain saw by the handle and pulled it from the bird. He had to use his foot to help release it, but after a few good tugs the blade came free. The swan carcass had fallen into several pieces; one of the wings was twitching slightly.

He thrust the blood covered saw into the hands of one of the white suited officers.

"Get that cleaned up," he said. "Bring the recovery team in, they should be here by now and get that thing sorted," he pointed to the pieces of swan.

The officer hesitated obviously uncomfortable with the order.

"Should we call the RSPCA sir?" he asked.

"I think it's beyond even their help now constable," retorted the sergeant.

"No sir what I mean is . . . are we not supposed to report it, because it's a swan sir, they are protected by the queen sir."

Pitcher held up his hands, turned the pages of an imaginary newspaper and read aloud.

"**Local Bobbie Murders Protected Bird**," he turned another page. "**Policeman in Wildlife Chain-Saw Massacre**."

He peered over the top of the invisible paper.

"I know sir, Sergeant Cygnet Slays Swan," the constable said through a grin.

Pitcher turned another page and read.

"**Young Constable on Charge for Insubordination**," he folded up the paper and tucked it under his arm. "Get it cleaned up," he barked.

They all heard the chain saw screech to a halt. Tom was the first to speak.

"Bloody hell that sounded a bit dodgy," he brushed the crumbs from his shirt and grabbed the binoculars. "I see someone. Bloody hell, I think there's been an accident he's covered in blood."

The binoculars were ripped from his hand.

"Hey," he said.

Russell had them, he looked through them for a second the thrust them back into Tom's hand and ran off around the bank. Saul dropped his sandwich and followed.

"Come on," Collin said. "We can go round the long way and meet the boat, they might need our help."

They trotted off heading in the opposite direction to Russell and Saul.

To Russell's surprise, Saul had caught up with him.

"Where are the others," Russell said without looking round.

"Gone the other way round to the jetty."

Russell stopped at the edge of the reeds he glanced around getting his bearings. They both headed into the reeds, but in different directions.

"Where are you going?" Russell shouted.

Saul paused and shouted back. "This way is quicker."

Without hesitation Russell followed his cousin, trusting Saul's contemporary knowledge of the lake. It was quicker and soon Russell recognised the path they were on, they sped along finally bursting into the clearing to find Pitcher lying on his back in the swans nest covered in blood, they rushed to his side.

"What are you doing here," Pitcher said with a smile.

Russell and Saul jumped back startled.

"We thought there had been an accident, is anyone hurt?" Russell said recovering himself.

"Very commendable lads, but no one is hurt, apart from the swan."

Saul and Russell knelt by the swan with Pitcher looking down. Saul was very upset and insisted that he be allowed to take care of it. Pitcher had no objection as long as it happened straight away. Using some of the plastic evidence bags Russell helped Saul collect all the pieces. With four large bags Saul and Russell left the nest and made their way back to the bank. Pitcher barely acknowledged them as they left because the recovery team had arrived there were now four white suited officers in the small clearing.

16:11

By the time Tom and Collin had reached the jetty the boat had landed. Judging by the laughter coming from the officers ahead it was obvious that no one was hurt. As they approached the police officers they slowed their pace and walked the last twenty yards. Brian was a good hundred yards behind, having chosen to take the bridge across the stream. The officers stopped laughing when they arrived and tried to stay serious, Collin looked at the chain saw covered in blood and feathers.

"What happened?" he said.

The officers suppressed a laugh. Brian caught up, took one look at the chain saw and burst out laughing.

"What's happened?" repeated Collin.

"He's killed that swan," Brian said wiping a tear from his eye.

"Ah that's not funny," Tom said.

"Let me tell you Tom," he said. "That bird was nasty and vicious."

"So is my bloody wife, but I wouldn't chop her up with a chain saw," he said.

Three Police officers took a professional look at Tom.

"I said I wouldn't chop her up," he was glad to see Russell walking up the bank.

Leaving the police officers, they walked back to Collin's bivvy where he announced that he was going to get a few hours kip through the afternoon. This seemed to be the order of the day and soon all four had retired for the rest of the day.

17:18

Saul scrapped out the last of the dirt with his bare hands, having to lie on the ground to reach the bottom of the grave. Satisfied that it would be deep enough he sat back on the soft cool earth that he had excavated. He had chosen a spot overlooking the reed bed, he thought it was appropriate and this was the only area of the bank that he could get a spade in because of the many roots. Nevertheless, it felt right that it should be him that buried it, up to him to give the swan the respect that an old adversary deserves.

He took three bags of bits and tossed them into the grave. He opened the last bag and pulled out the section of the bird which included the head and one wing. He placed this in the hole and arranged it as best he could with the head facing forward. Using his hands he started to fill the grave. When the bird was almost covered, when only the swans head was exposed, he stopped he moved back and stood with his head bowed. He patted his pockets.

"That's very respectful of you Saul, well done."

The voice made him jump, but he did not show it.

"Hello sergeant Pitcher, do you have a coin Mr Pitcher?"

"Yes I think so," he rummaged in his pocket and handed over a pound coin.

Saul took it and placed it gently under the swans head, then continued to fill the hole with the soft earth. Pitcher smiled and helped fill the grave in silence. They walked back to the house together.

"I don't know much about burying animals, but that was a nice thing you did back there Saul, with the coin."

Saul was a bit surprised and embarrassed.

"Oh, um, thank you Mr Pitcher I can give you the pound back if you want I have it at home."

"No not at all," he laughed and ruffled Saul's hair.

Pitcher returned the now gleaming chain saw and took the opportunity to give Saul a lift home. On his return to the lake there was little to do other than supervise the team of officers. By this time word was out around the local village, it never took long. Three or four locals and one reporter had already been turned away at the gate. He wanted to be away from here before any national reporters started to arrive.

19:06

A shiny blue helicopter hovered low above the lake. A
man was leaning out of the side door with a large
television camera. Pitcher was in the garden shouting into
his radio.

"Move him or nick him I don't care which, just get rid
of him."

He could not believe his luck, another ten minutes
and they would have been finished. The last of his officers
retreated to their vans and cars they started to leave. Pitcher
walked back down to the lake over the stream and round
to where Russell and Collin were bivvied up. As he walked
along the bank the helicopter pulled up and away from the
lake.

He arrived at the camp to find Russell and Collin sitting
out with the kettle on he sat with them and filled them in

over a cup of tea. He was telling Russell about Saul burying the swan when Russell cut in.

"Did he put a coin under the head?" he asked.

"Why yes he did," exclaimed Pitcher. "In fact I gave him a pound. How did you know that, is it some kind of tradition?"

"No, it just makes it easier to find," Russell said.

Pitcher looked confused.

"With a metal detector; he will wait until next year and dig up the skull," Russell said.

Pitcher frowned.

"Damm it," he said. "I should have given him a penny."

20:08

C ollin and Russell said their good-byes to Pitcher when
he headed back to the station. They cleaned up and
strolled the long way round to Brian and Tom. There was
a light breeze on the water the air was fresh and scented.
The evening sun was starting to get fat and low. One or two
thin clouds had formed on the horizon. The frenzied buzz
of insects was louder by the waters edge. They stopped by
a patch of lilies to watch a large shoal of Rudd and Crusion
carp picking bugs from the surface.

"If only I had my pole with me, some of those Rudd are
topping the pound mark," Collin said excitedly.

All around the lake there was an intense activity Collin
looked up to see half a dozen mallards swing round to land
in the middle of the lake. Way off in the distance Russell

could make out a few geese heading their way. Collin shook his head.

"I never noticed that there were no other ducks on the lake," he said. "Apart from the two coots, do you think the word has got out that the wicked swan of the lake is dead?"

"The evidence speaks for itself. Word travels fast in the bird world," Russell said and laughed aloud as even more birds descended on the lake.

20:20

They met up with the others and decided on tactics over their last meal. Tom had managed to rustle up pasta shells with sauce, even managing to produce a small handful of grated cheese to throw on top.

"I can see why you go fishing with Tom," Collin said.

He was addressing Brian who just grinned with a mouthful of food.

After dinner, they all sat back with a beer. It was like looking at a different lake, there were now hundreds of water birds on the surface. The wind had dropped away to nothing, but the entire surface of the lake was in constant movement. The noise was insane, constant jabbering, quacking and honking. Mallards laughed continuously, a gaggle of twenty white geese had boarded the island they were busy fending off tufted pirates who were making a stand for the southern tip. A large flock of Canadian geese executed an impressive, co-ordinated landing and then made for the open bank near the old jetty. Coots and crested grebes had appeared along with more varieties of duck. Birds were heading into the reeds seeking out prime real estate.

20:45

As the last of the light started to go, a lone swan appeared over the tree line coming straight out of the fading sun. There was a flurry of activity on the lake as all birds rushed to the edge into the reeds and under overhanging bushes seeking cover. Several ducks left the water right in front of the fishermen rushing past to crouch behind Tom's bivvy. As suddenly as it had started it stopped, all activity on the lake died away. The anglers leaned silently forward in their seats the swan circled one more time then landed on the rapidly calming water and drew to a halt.

The cob looked around the lake and swallowed loudly. This was a little uncomfortable. He tried a smile.

Looking up he was very glad to see his partner circle round and land next to him. As soon as the second swan came into view all activity recommenced, the men relaxed back into their chairs.

"This lake is weird," Brian said and pointed across the water with his beer. "There's no chance of fishing the island undetected, in fact we will be lucky to get a line in without hitting a duck."

"What are we going to do now?" Collin said.

They all looked at Russell, who was sitting back with his eyes closed soaking up the new sounds on the lake. They spent the next few hours walking around the lake looking for signs of carp. However, there were so many birds scooting about that it was almost impossible. Eventually they worked their way round to the stream Brian was not keen on the stepping-stones so he elected to go down to the bridge.

"As long as you wait for me over there," he pointed to the other bank.

"Yeah sure mate," Tom said.

"Ok see you in a minute," Brian said and trotted down stream toward the bridge.

23:08

As he approached the weir he slowed and stopped at the start of the bridge. He looked around with slight trepidation remembering the night before. How different it all looked now. The moon was rising above the tree line. It looked huge. Logic told him that it was always the same size, but given all that had happened in the last twenty four hours he was quite prepared to believe that it was coming down to get him. He was about to continue when something caught his eye in the water. It took a while to realise what he was looking at. In the water a few yards from the bridge was a very large fish, only visible because its back was out of the water. Slowly he descended into a crouch peering through the undergrowth he could clearly see the black back and dorsal fin in the moonlight. Further back he made out the tip of the tail; he guessed it to be about twenty-five pounds.

It was not the only fish to have taken refuge in the stream. As he watched he could identify at least four other carp. He decided not to cross the bridge so he retreated to the stepping-stones hoping that the guys had waited for him.

They had and a few minutes later all four of them were hiding amongst the ferns and grass watching.

"How long do you think they will stay here Russ?" Tom asked, in a hushed voice.

"Hard to say maybe till dawn, there is a lot going on across the lake."

"Do you think we could catch one?" Collin said.

"Not from here that's for sure, these are waiting carp not feeding carp. When they move we may be able to tempt one from the head of the stream, but it will be a one shot wonder. As soon as one of us hooks a fish the rest of the shoal will scatter. I suggest that we set up one rod each and cover the stream head, two on each side."

"Do you think we could catch one there?" Collin said.

Russell just shrugged his shoulders in a non-committal way. They pulled back and headed for the bivvies.

An hour later they returned with enough kit to last until dawn. Tom and Brian had walked the long way round having decided that they stood the best chance on the other bank. As they arrived, Russell was just returning from a quick check on the carp. From the far side of the stream Russell gave them the thumbs up.

The four men picked their swims there was no argument as to who fished where because everyone seemed to have a different idea of which the best place to hook a giant. Brian waited to see where Russell was going to fish then found a similar swim on his side of the stream. Russell had chosen a spot further out of the stream where the bank rounded into the lake, he seemed to be perched on some sort of fallen log, it was hard to tell in the failed light. Brian squeezed himself through some thick low bushes to find a small narrow clearing large enough to set a chair and a rod. Most of the clearing was screened from the lake by tall grass, leaving only a short open gap at the end, perfect for the rod tip. He guessed that Russell or Saul had developed this swim over the years. This boosted him with confidence.

Tom lay on his stomach and peered through the long bank-side grass and gazed across the water. He noted that the surface weed was quite deep here, stretching out for at least ten feet from the bank. He also noticed that a passage had been forced through it. He shuffled along the bank using the reflection of the moon to highlight the weed; there was definitely a channel. He shuffled a little more and found the entrance. As the weed ended, the channel opened into clear water. This was where he would lay his bait. He glanced across to the other bank he squinted and could just make out Collin laying on his front peering out over the water. Tom reached for his mobile.

Collin jumped, startled by the vibrating phone, he was quick to answer. It was Tom and he was laughing.

"Have you found a channel in the weed," Collin said. "I have just found the same thing, but we will have to sit quite a way back there's not much cover along the edge."

He rolled over and pocketed the phone as soon as he did so he got a text from Russ, 'get set then meet in the middle', it said.

A short while later he walked up stream. Russell was talking to Tom on a mobile. Collin looked across and could just make out Brian and Tom on the opposite bank, Russell was hanging up.

"What's happening then Russ?"

"Everyone is ready, just waiting for the carp to move, how about you?"

"Yeah, found a channel in the weed, I will drop in a couple of pva bags at the end of it. Then I will free-line a couple of peanuts on a short hair, inside a small quick melt pva bag. And I added a few nips of heavy metal to pin down the last three feet. What do you think?"

"Sounds good, it's pretty much what I would be doing in that swim. Apart from the pva bags of course and the putty, maybe only one peanut, what size hook you on?"

"Size six Raptor."

"Think I would go to an eight or ten, short shank with a long soft hair to counter blow back. Why are you using peanuts?"

"Because that's what your cousin said he used."

"But didn't he tell you that he lied and that he had never used peanuts before?"

There was a pause.

"Yes he did, but I'm not so sure he was telling the truth."

"Why not?"

"Because when I asked what the real bait was, he said that there was no special bait. I know when I'm being lied to, however well it's done."

"He was lying, but not about the peanuts."

"I knew it: what?"

"He lied about the bait, there is a special bait, but it's not peanuts."

Collin clapped a hand over his face.

"Rollocks," he said. "Did he tell you what it was?"

"No."

Collin waited a second then asked.

"Do you know what the bait is?"

"Yes."

"What is it?"

Russell handed him a small plastic bag, Collin took it looking confused, he opened it and sniffed the contents.

"Cheese?"

"Yes."

"How did you find out?"

Russell tapped the side of this nose and Collin tipped the bag into his palm; there were four squares of firm cheese.

"Where did you get them?"

"I grabbed most of the cheese from Tom before we had dinner."

"Do the others know?"

"Yes and I gave them the same two cubes each, so it's all square. Use them or not, it's up to you I'm going to see if the fish are moving. Coming?"

"Sure, meet you there in a minute I want to take a second look at my rig."

05:45

They had taken turns watching the fish over the last few hours in between naps. As first light started to break on the horizon, they each got a text from Tom 'carp on move' it read.

Tom got back to his rod well ahead of the carp he guessed that they would take about twenty minutes or so to reach his swim and the same for Collin who was opposite him. He swung out his line with its single cheese hook bait into what he thought would be the optimum spot. There was no wind so the ripples were free to extend themselves across the water. He teased the line until he was satisfied with the lay he stayed crouched by the edge looking and listening. A couple of pigeons had decided to have a row behind him and somewhere above him a redstart that was going off like a bite alarm. He zipped his fleece all the way up to keep out the dawn chill, he waited and watched. He glanced across the stream he could see Collin doing the same on the other side. They grinned at each other in the dawn light. Tom ducked further back from the edge there was nothing to do other than wait.

Brian pointed the rod tip due east at the first glimmer of rising sun.

"Ok," he whispered. "What now?"

In his Bluetooth earpiece Russell gave him some more instruction. He manoeuvred the rod until only a foot of tip stuck out over the water. More instruction came through the earpiece.

"Get out of it, your having a laugh," he replied. "Ok, if you're sure,"

He lowered the bait into the water directly under the tip then pulled his rod back leaving a very slack line. It was barely a couple of feet deep it was hard for him to believe that a carp would come this close to the bank.

"I am really not sure about this Russ," he sat back in his low chair watching the slack line at the rod tip.

Russell tucked his mobile away, he did not cast out just watched and waited.

06:14

Each man lay covered with a silvery layer of dew as they waited motionless and silent. No one was using buzzers; nobody was even using rod rests.

Brian yawned and the line twitched. His jaw snapped shut he was instantly alert. It twitched again, he leaned forward in the chair his heart starting to thump.

Collin's rod tip quivered, the line pulling a little tighter, he sat up. The line slackened again then twitched violently. Collin was out of his chair and crouched next to the rod his hand hovering above it. The line slackened again.

Across the water he saw Tom run forward and strike, his rod tip ripped down. Tom was in.

The water between them moved, deep bow waves appeared as several large fish darted out from the weed. Collin looked down to see his own line pulling away he

186

struck into nothing. He reeled in laid his rod down amongst the long grass and ran down to the stepping-stones. As he ran he pulled his phone from his pocket.

Tom's heart felt like a hammer against his ribs, he could not believe that the line had shot away so lightning fast. It felt like a heavy fish. It rose to and crashed on the surface before diving again stripping line heading out into open water. Tom applied a bit more pressure.

Russell got the call from Collin telling him what he already knew. He watched as several fish dashed out of the stream carving deep bow waves, he decided to call Brian as he made his way to Tom.

The phone made Brian jump he was still wearing the hands free unit while watching his line intently. He slowly raised his hand and touched the earpiece.

"Ok Russ," he said quietly. "I'll be there in a minute."

Russell joined Collin behind Tom, who was trying to control what looked like a heavy fish, the rod bent over and the carp was slowly cruising up stream.

"I can't seem to turn it," Tom said and added a bit more side strain.

"Careful Tom, careful, not too much," Collin said. "What line have you got on the reel?"

"12lb soft steel, it's turning, it's coming back."

The fish was indeed slowly coming to the bank. Russell was there with the net, he waited patiently crouched on the bank, he scooped forwards with confidence netting the fish and a fair amount of weed, he pulled the heavy net back, detached the handle and struggled to lift the net from the water.

They huddled around the unhooking mat as the weed parted, a selection of water fleas and boatmen sprang from the net. Minnows and small fry were caught up in the scoop along with even more weed. Under that they found a large common passively lying in the bottom, but not that large. When they finally cleared the weed, it was a bit disappointing. Russell slipped the common into a weigh sling and Collin held up the scales.

"Well it's not the monster, but it goes eighteen," Tom said. "And I think that puts me in the lead for the most weight, a few pounds ahead of Brian."

Collin looked all around.

"Where's Brian?" He said.

From further down the bank they could faintly hear Brian shouting for help. Russell left the other two to return the fish while he ran toward the distant pleas for assistance.

Brian was up to his knees in the water in front of his swim his rod bent double and the drag on the reel screaming continuously, he quickly glanced back.

"Russ, it tore off so fast it nearly took the rod, I had to jump in to catch the end of it. I can't stop it," he shouted. "And I can't reach my net from here, but somehow I don't think I will need it yet."

Russell followed Brian's line; the fish was now in open water heading, at a fair rate, toward the island, Brian pulled back on the rod trying to slow the fish. There was a deep wide swell out in the open water as the fish turned on the surface.

Tom and Collin arrived.

"Wow," Tom said when he saw the swell. "That is a big fish."

Russell had forced his way through the bushes down to Brian's swim and was now next to him in the water with the net ready. The carp changed tack kiting off to Brian's right, the sudden turn took Brian by surprise, for a few tense seconds there was slack line. The three spectators groaned in despair then cheered when the line tightened, the fish was still on.

The next few minutes were fraught with tricky turns and sudden runs, but Brian was slowly taking control, yard by torturous yard he gained on the monster. When he had retrieved twenty yards or so the fish bolted again, stripping away all that Brian had gained and then some. Back to square one, all Brian's attempts to stop the fish were failing.

Everyone was silent other than the occasional collective gasp as the fish made determined runs toward various snags and deeper water. Once again, Brian took the upper hand and started to gain line. As the fish came in it started to pull in smaller and smaller circles and made only half-hearted runs, but it stayed firmly on the bottom.

The first rays of the sun hit the lake bathing the whole scene in a warm orange glow. Within a few seconds it became a fierce dazzling lightshow on the broken water before them. Russell and Brian were blinded by the reflections each of them threw up a hand to protect their eyes. The carp knew: it moved fast shooting to the surface and broke through clearing the water only a few feet in front of Brian. Taken by surprise at the sudden move Brian staggered, all control was lost, the line was slack the hook was spat.

The true size of the carp became apparent Tom and Collin gasped. The fish had a thick broad head and a wide expanse of copper flank, pectoral fins the size of a man's hand followed by a massive tail. The carp twisted in the air, the sun hit the copper flank and just for a second it blazed like hot metal. The fire was quenched a spray of water hit Brian full in the face.

They were stunned, no one moved, they all watched the huge fish slide away beneath the ruptured surface. It rolled once more on the surface then slipped away forever.

Water dripped off Brian's nose, in the distance the mallards were laughing.

"Fucking fuck it," Brian shouted and threw down his rod; it sank in the shallow water.

"If you ask me," Russell said. "That was a huge fish."

"Really, over thirty?" he said after a pause.

Russell patted him on the back.

"Easily; come on lets go home."

17:21

Tom watched Brian emerge from the back door of the pub. He was laughing with two girls sitting just inside. He carried four pints on a small tray toward their bench at the end of the urban pub garden, Tom wondered if either of the girls was Betty. According to the bench graffiti she would do it for a pint of Stella.

Russell had asked Tom, Collin and Brian to meet him at the pub it was two weeks since they had returned from the lake.

Brian arrived and distributed the beers.

"So why are we all here then Russ?" he said.

"Thank you Brian," Russell said, as he took the beer. "I got a letter from Saul and he sent some photos."

Russell tossed a thick envelope on to the bench; Collin picked it up and shook out the contents.

There were twenty-five 10 x 8 colour prints of themselves. He spread them on the table, Tom, Collin and Brian each reached for their own pics. There were a few close ups taken with the zoom lens, shots of Collin Tom and Brian, none of the guys looked good. Brian took a long look at the picture taken when he had entered the den. It was one picture with five images of him falling to the ground, each image showing a new startled face.

"How did he do this Russ?" Brian said.

"There was a sensor in the den and I guess it opened the shutter on a single frame for a few seconds while the flashes went off. It's quite easy to do."

Brian pulled out the final shot Saul had taken of him, the picture that he had taken just after saving him from the swan. The man looking out from the close up was hardly recognisable. It was like looking at a picture of himself as a destitute old man that had some how travelled back in time. There was mud ingrained into every crease he had a defeated look in his wild staring eyes. He looked closer and he could clearly make out Saul's silhouette reflected in his own eyes and there just behind it, he could see the swan.

"Mind if I keep this one Russ?" Brian said.

"Sure."

"I notice that there are none of you Russ," Collin said. "No hang on, what's this."

Collin stared in wonder at the shot of Russell wrestling the swan. It was obvious that Saul had a keen eye for a good shot. Even though the picture was taken in haste, he had managed to capture the moment when the swan had slashed Russell's face. Its wings were at full stretch it looked huge even compared to Russell's gangling frame.

"This should be in an exhibition Russ; I have never seen anything like this before," Collin said in wonder.

Tom sat back with one of his own pictures, the moment when he had lost the second big fish on the very first day.

"You're right Cole, just look at the detail here. I remember the moment when I lost that fish. He must have been on the island all the time we were there on day one. Still it could be worse," he ventured. "We could be all over the internet."

"Actually Tom," Russell said. "Saul has got his own web site so it's a safe bet that we are."

They all looked at Russell and Tom started laughing.

"Hey, now you mention bets what about the money?" Brian said. "I believe you have the final score Tom."

Tom pulled the piece of paper from his back pocket.

"Yes I have and the biggest fish goes to Brian with a 25lb mirror, well done sir, but the most weight goes to me, hooray, with 73lb so hand over the money."

They each gave Tom their twenty-five quid and in turn, they all gave Brian ten.

"Easy money," Tom said as he slipped the notes into his wallet.

"I still say that we should have counted fish under fifteen pound, if we had I would have won hands down. Just as long as you all know that," Collin said trying to regain a little self-esteem.

"There was one extra picture I asked him to send," Russell said. "This one is for you Brian, do you recognise this fish?"

Russell handed over a copy of the photo that he had first seen on the cork board in Saul's den. It was the picture that Saul had taken from the lightning tree.

Brian's mouth dropped open.

"Yes, that's it. That is the fish I lost, how big?"

"Upper thirty for sure," Russell said.

Brian was looking lovingly at the photo; he touched the carp on the nose.

"I'm coming back for you," he said.

He looked up at the other three.

"We are going back, aren't we?"

42lb 4oz Kent

The author

C arp fishing is not a sport, it's not a pastime and it's not a hobby. It is an all consuming passion that drives men away from warm beds, good pubs and beautiful women.

Will Martin has been described as a fanatical carp fisherman; he has also been described as an idiot, usually by beautiful women, pub landlords and makers of warm beds. He has been fishing for over 40 years, not continuously of course although he does have the crazy ambition of fishing for a whole year.

He drifted through all the usual stages of a lifelong fisherman, from tiddler bashing on the Chase in Dagenham through to carp stalking on distant backwaters in Norfolk and Oxford. Pike fishing, specimen roach tench and big bream have all featured in his career, but since the late seventies carp have held a special place in his heart and for the last 15 years have been a small obsession. He is often found with his fishing partner, friend and little brother Steve, with whom he has shared many long road trips fishing across the south of England.

A keen amateur writer with a love of the English language Will started keeping, as many fishermen do, a journal of his fishing trips. This love of writing and his inherent sense of humour resulted in this book. He is currently writing part two of this fishing adventure and plans to publish next year.

As every fisherman knows it not always about what you catch, it's about being there. Will is happiest when surrounded by green overlooking wind ruffled water. His best carp to date is a 42lb 4oz mirror taken from a lake in Kent, although he will be the first to say that size is irrelevant and catching nothing is just an occupational hazard. Will is, at this moment, either fishing, planning to go fishing, writing about fishing or dreaming about it.

Fanatic or idiot? It depends on whether you are a beautiful woman with your own pub and a warm bed, or a fellow fisherman.

22lb Norfolk

33lb 3oz Oxford

Little Brother Steve 27lb 12oz Oxford

Three seconds later